Teaching Faculty How to Use Technology

Recent Titles in the ACE Series on Higher Education

Teaching Faculty How to Use Technology
Best Practices from Leading Institutions

Rhonda M. Epper
and
A. W. (Tony) Bates

AMERICAN COUNCIL ON EDUCATION ★
ORYX PRESS ★
Series on Higher Education
2001

The rare Arabian Oryx is believed to have inspired the myth of the unicorn. This desert antelope became virtually extinct in the early 1960s. At that time, several groups of international conservationists arranged to have nine animals sent to the Phoenix Zoo to be the nucleus of a captive breeding herd. Today, the Oryx population is over 1,000, and over 500 have been returned to the Middle East.

Library of Congress Cataloging-in-Publication Data

Teaching faculty how to use technology : best practices from leading institutions / [edited by] Rhonda M. Epper and A.W. (Tony) Bates.
    p. cm.—(American Council on Education/Oryx Press series on higher education)
    Includes bibliographical references and index.
    ISBN 1-57356-386-2 (alk. paper)
    1. Educational technology—Study and teaching (Higher).   2. Computer-assisted instruction.   3. Teachers—Training of.   4. Teachers—In-service training.   I. Epper, Rhonda.   II. Bates, Tony, 1939–   III. Series.
LB1028.3.T38   2001
378.1'734—dc21   2001032156

British Library Cataloguing in Publication Data is available.

Library of Congress Catalog Card Number: 2001032156
ISBN: 1-57356-386-2

First published in 2001

Oryx Press, 88 Post Road West, Westport, CT 06881
An imprint of Greenwood Publishing Group, Inc.
www.oryxpress.com

Printed in the United States of America

∞

The paper used in this book complies with the Permanent Paper Standard issued by the National Information Standards Organization (Z39.48-1984).

10 9 8 7 6 5 4 3 2 1

CONTENTS

CONTRIBUTOR
PROFILES

Rhonda M. Epper is a special consultant for the California State University, Office of the Chancellor, serving on the founding staff for the MERLOT Project (Multimedia Educational Resource for Learning and Online Teaching). MERLOT (www.merlot.org) is an organization made up of colleges, universities, state systems of higher education, and private college consortia throughout the United States and Canada. Its mission is to improve the effectiveness of teaching and learning by expanding the quantity and quality of peer-reviewed online learning materials available to faculty. Prior to her work on MERLOT, Dr. Epper was a project director with the State Higher Education Executive Officers (SHEEO). In this role, she worked with senior staff and chief executives of state higher education coordinating and governing boards on public policy issues, such as governance, academic program policy, and technology policy and planning.

Dr. Epper has published articles on the implementation of instructional technologies in higher education in *The Journal of Higher Education* (1997), *Planning for Higher Education* (1998), *Trusteeship* (1996), and *Change Magazine* (1999), in addition to several book chapters. She also published numerous reports while at SHEEO in the areas of academic program policy and distance learning policy. Dr. Epper completed her Ph.D. in higher education administration at the University of Denver in 1996. She received an MBA from the University of Denver, and a BBA in finance from the University of Texas at Austin.

A. W. (Tony) Bates is one of the world's leading experts in the use of technology for university-level teaching. He is one of the world's 10 most quoted authors in the field of distance education and has almost 30 years' experience in applying, managing, and researching the application of technologies to higher education teaching. Dr. Bates is the director of distance education and technology at the University of British Columbia (UBC), where his unit has over 40 courses in production using the World Wide Web or CD-ROMs for course delivery. Prior to joining UBC in 1995, he was executive director, strategic planning, research, and information technology at the Open Learning Agency of British Columbia. He came to Canada after 20 years as a founding member of the British Open University, where he was professor of educational media research.

He is the author of several seminal works on the application of technology to teaching, including the award-winning *Technology, Open Learning and Distance Education* (Routledge, 1995), and, most recently, *Managing Technological Change* (Jossey-Bass, 2000). Dr. Bates has worked as a consultant on the use of technology for university teaching for the World Bank, UNESCO, the British Council, the Canadian International Development Agency, several U.S. state higher education commissions, and for universities and government ministries of education in over 30 countries. He received his Ph.D. in educational administration from the University of London, England, in 1972.

CONTRIBUTORS—AMERICAN PRODUCTIVITY & QUALITY CENTER (APQC), HOUSTON, TEXAS

Marisa Martin Brown is the benchmarking manager for the American Productivity & Quality Center's (APQC) Collaborative Learning Group. Since joining the Center in January 1996, she has been integrally involved with all aspects of consortium benchmarking studies. Brown was also involved in the creation and establishment of APQC's services for education institutions. She is currently responsible for overseeing all the consortium benchmarking offerings of the Center.

Brown has managed some of APQC's largest consortium learning forums in the education arena, including Technology-Mediated Learning and Faculty Instructional Development: Supporting Faculty Use of Technology in Teaching. She has also managed studies in Developmental Education, Creating Electronic Student and Customer Services, Assessing Learning Outcomes, Measuring Institutional Performance Outcomes, and Institutional Budgeting. Additionally, she has facilitated benchmarking studies focusing on the needs of individual organizations, including a study on the topic of best practices in adult learner focused institutions.

Prior to joining APQC, Brown received extensive training in ISO9000 quality system implementation. She earned her MBA with highest honors from the University of Texas at Austin Graduate School of Business, where she was a Dean's Award recipient. She also earned her BBA with highest honors from the University of Texas at Austin, majoring in finance and honors business.

Ron Webb, a director within APQC, is in charge of the Collaborative Learning and Information Services Groups. The Collaborative Learning Group conducts group benchmarking projects for APQC customers, while Information Services works to assist both internal APQC groups and external customers in the proper use of publicly available sources of information. Through these two groups, APQC is able to generate an enormous amount of best-practice content for its customers.

In addition to these product groups, Webb heads an internal APQC group focused on integrating all APQC's products and services that focus on the processes impacting an organization's customers, such as marketing, sales, and customer service. The goal of this group is to ensure that APQC has best practices available to its customers to assist them in acquiring and servicing their customers.

Prior to joining APQC, Webb worked in the healthcare field and has a strong knowledge base in that industry. Ron holds a masters of urban planning degree from Texas A&M University with an emphasis in health systems planning, and a bachelor of science degree from Texas A&M University in community health.

CONTRIBUTOR—BELLEVUE COMMUNITY COLLEGE, BELLEVUE, WASHINGTON

Kae R. Hutchison is principal of Hutchison Consulting. Dr. Hutchison consults with higher education institutions on organizational and staff development. She held a series of increasingly responsible positions at Bellevue Community College (BCC), culminating her 34 years there as special assistant to the president for institutional effectiveness and dean of instructional administration. Her instructional administrative responsibilities included faculty professional development, enrollment and budget management, and new program development.

A founding faculty member of BCC, Dr. Hutchison began her educational career in music, serving as music program chair and creative arts division chair. For 18 years, she led the college's continuing education program, developing it to the largest in the state community college system and making it known for its breadth, excellent instruction, and leading edge computer programs. In 1981, she helped establish an intensive English institute for international students at the college, a program that brings over 350 students to BCC annually. Dr. Hutchison established the first computer lab at BCC and has been a leader in adopting computer technology for her programs and work.

Dr. Hutchison's doctoral work examined the professional development of community and technical college administrators in Washington State. She has followed up on the needs identified in her work by developing state-level professional development activities for new and experienced administrators through the Association for Washington Community & Technical College Administrators, including programs for new and experienced administrators. In 1998, Dr. Hutchison was the driving force behind BCC's successful application to the Association for Productivity & Quality Center (APQC) to be a benchmark college for its approaches to faculty professional development, with emphasis on faculty use of technology.

CONTRIBUTORS—CALIFORNIA STATE UNIVERSITY, CENTER FOR DISTRIBUTED LEARNING

Gerard L. Hanley received his Ph.D. in psychology from the State University of New York at Stony Brook in 1984 and became a faculty member in the Department of Psychology at California State University, Long Beach. He has published or presented over 80 research papers on issues concerning cognition, learning, memory, neuroscience, clinical and community psychology, educational processes and assessment, critical thinking, industrial and organizational psychology, human factors, knowledge engineering, software engineering, and systems engineering.

At CSU, Long Beach, he was the director of the Center for Faculty Development for six years and director of the Office of Strategic Planning for three years. He continues to be the director of the Center for Usability in Design and Assessment (CUDA), which is a research, service, and instruction center for designing and implementing methodologies for evaluating the effectiveness and usability of technology. CUDA has acquired over 40 grants and contracts from educational institutions, government agencies, and private industry since its inception in 1996.

Dr. Hanley's current position is senior director for Academic Technology Services for the California State University System. The focus of his recent efforts is building and sustaining online communities and resources to improve the effectiveness of teaching and learning in higher education. One major project under his leadership is MERLOT (Multimedia Educational Resources for Learning and Online Teaching)—an integrated and multidisciplinary online community supported by a consortium of 23 systems and institutions of higher education.

Charles Schneebeck is a special consultant with the California State University (CSU) on the MERLOT (Multimedia Educational Resource for Learning and Online Teaching) project. As one of the founders of MERLOT, Schneebeck provides strategic guidance and development of partnerships between MERLOT and commercial and nonprofit organizations.

He is former director of the CSU Center for Distributed Learning, which creates strategies for the development and sharing of electronic learning materials that are both scalable and sustainable. In addition to launching the MERLOT project, the Center for Distributed Learning formed a partnership with Addison-Wesley Longman Publishing Company to develop Biology Labs Online, a series of laboratory simulations for use on the World Wide Web.

Schneebeck served as director of academic computing services at California State University, Long Beach, from 1990 to 1996, and as director of academic computing at Fullerton College from 1984 to 1990. He was on the biology faculty at Fullerton College from 1969 to 1984.

CONTRIBUTORS—COLLÈGE BORÉAL, ONTARIO, CANADA

David Fasciano is currently a faculty member in the School of Business and Technology in the Information Systems program at Collège Boréal. He served as director of mobile computing from June 1998 to June 1999 and was responsible for coordinating the full-scale implementation of Collège Boréal's mobile computing initiative.

Louise Gervais-Guy has a licence en orientation scolaire et professionnelle from Laval University. During most of her professional life, she has worked in the areas related to personal, educational, and career counseling, disability issues, and development of learning support resources. Gervais-Guy has collaborated in the portable computer integration project as coordinator of technical support services. Before returning to counseling, she spent a year developing learning support services for Boreal's online courses project.

Daniel Gingras has been involved in college administration since 1990. He has worked with teams in student services and directed "La Fondation du Collège Boréal" in its campaign that raised over $5 million for student bursaries. He has been involved in e-learning initiatives since 1999, directing e-learning development and implementation. He has been successful in obtaining funds and developing partnerships for e-learning from the local to the national levels.

Raymond Guy has been involved in instructional design and faculty support since early 1997. He founded the faculty support center, "La Cuisine," at Collège Boréal and now coordinates instructional design and production activities in the e-learning/distributed learning initiatives. He has been evaluating teaching and learning tools and providing support in their integration in learning activities. Prior to working in the field of e-learning, Guy has been developing and teaching in programs in natural resource management and tourism. His 10 years of teaching experience in the college environment have provided him with the opportunity to experiment with video and audioconferencing as well as with some Web-based applications. He will be teaching a course on instructional design as associate professor at the Institut Universitaire de Technologie de Toulon, France, in June 2001.

Renée Hallée has worked at Collège Boréal since 1995. She has been involved in the administrative fields of customer service and registrar office. Also, she has been involved in the delivery of distance education, mostly in terms of providing logistic support for learners. As manager of continuing education for four years, she has been involved with the electronic learning environment regarding the aspects of learner file administration and user services.

Chantal Pollock is a graduate of the University of Toronto (M.Ed.). She has worked in the college system in a variety of positions. At Collège Boréal, she set up the distance education program, which included over 130 courses distributed over seven campuses and using the technologies of videoconferencing, audioconferencing, and audiographics conferencing. She has also overseen the transformation of classroom practices among faculty, mainly the transition from traditional to nontraditional teaching. Presently, as dean of learning and support services, she is responsible for innovative student services offered over seven campuses using many technologies.

CONTRIBUTORS—UNIVERSITY OF CENTRAL FLORIDA, ORLANDO

Joel L. Hartman is vice provost for information technologies and resources at the University of Central Florida (UCF) in Orlando. As the university's CIO, he has overall responsibility for library, computing, networking, telecommunications, media services, and distributed learning technology activities.

Before joining UCF in 1995, Hartman was CIO at Bradley University (1967 to 1995), where his career included several senior information technology management positions. Hartman has been an information technology consultant to both public and private sector organizations, and has been active in the development of state educational telecommunications policy and resources in Illinois and Florida. He has served and held offices on numerous state, regional, and national IT committees in areas including public broadcasting, distributed learning, and networking. He currently serves on the EDUCAUSE Board and the NLII Planning Committee, and is a frequent presenter at professional conferences.

Hartman received his bachelor's and master's degrees in journalism and communication from the University of Illinois, Urbana-Champaign; he is completing doctoral work at the University of Central Florida.

Barbara Truman-Davis is the director of course development and Web services (CD&WS) at the University of Central Florida (UCF). CD&WS supports UCF's online degrees and programs, and has responsibility for faculty, staff, and course development. The unit is also responsible for campus-wide Web activities, including the university's main Web site.

CD&WS is composed of teams of instructional designers, digital media specialists, Web developers called Techrangers, Web analysts, video services specialists, and software engineers who collaborate to produce multimedia and Web-based resources.

Truman-Davis holds a master's degree in instructional systems design from UCF and she is completing doctoral studies in curriculum and instruction, specializing in Web-based learning. She helped create UCF's first fully online course with Dr. Steven Sorg in early 1996, and was tapped to head the university's faculty development program for online program development in June 1996. Her research interests include computer-supported collaborative learning and virtual teams.

CONTRIBUTOR—VIRGINIA TECH, BLACKSBURG

Anne H. Moore is the director of information technology initiatives at Virginia Tech. Drawing on Virginia Tech's strengths in information technology, Dr. Moore is responsible for building partnerships within the university and with other organizations that assist in meeting modern needs for technology in society. She oversees the university's Learning Technologies operation, heads the Center for Innovation in Learning, which provides grants to faculty for integrating technology into teaching in strategic curricular areas, and directs the Executive Forum in Information Technology, which encourages public discussion on current technology issues. She also chairs the Electronic Campus of Virginia, a cooperative of public and private institutions focused on providing distance learning to citizens.

PREFACE

For several decades college administrators have pursued the promises of technology-enhanced education. In the quest for these promises (namely, better teaching, more learning, at lower costs), they have overcome exceedingly difficult financial and organizational obstacles. Networks have been built, computers bought, and software installed. Huge investments in campus and statewide technical infrastructures have been made. But the most daunting challenge in implementing technology in college teaching is still ahead of us: the development and training of faculty.

For institutions to fully benefit from their investments in technology, faculty must use the technology available to improve their teaching and their students' learning. For years faculty known as "early adopters" experimented with technology in the classroom and at a distance. Now, as more and more "mainstream" faculty are using technology in their teaching, institutions must prepare to meet their demands for both equipment and training. Campuses across North America and around the world are putting resources into faculty development initiatives, which come in many forms. Examples include workshops, faculty resource centers, technical and pedagogical assistance, and even online courses designed for faculty who want to teach online courses. But as faculty interest in teaching with technology continues to escalate, even the largest and wealthiest institutions will be challenged to meet the development and training needs.

This book addresses the ways in which several institutions are responding to the growing demand for faculty support in the use of instructional technology. The chapters represent the state of events at each institution in 2001, but the book is largely based on a study conducted in 1998 by the State Higher

Education Executive Officers (SHEEO) and the American Productivity & Quality Center (APQC) entitled "Faculty Instructional Development: Supporting Faculty Use of Technology in Teaching." This seven-month study was designed to identify and examine organizations that could be considered "best practice" in helping faculty integrate technology into the teaching and learning process. Over 100 higher education institutions and 20 business and government organizations participated in the study as sponsors, "best practice" candidates, or "best practice" organizations. Although it may be impossible to select a set of institutions and declare them the "best" in anything, we believe the institutions involved in the SHEEO/APQC study have developed strong and effective programs that can inform those who may be launching down a similar path. Therefore, we asked those who are deep in the trenches of faculty development programs at these outstanding institutions to tell their stories— not just their successes, but also their missteps and how they have overcome the greatest challenges to helping faculty implement technology in their teaching.

The book is intended primarily for key academic decision makers within colleges and universities, including presidents, academic vice presidents, deans, department heads, and faculty leadership. It is also aimed at policy leaders such as board of trustee members, state boards for higher education, and system-level administrators and their staffs. This book will also be of particular interest to professionals in instructional technology support areas, such as faculty development, centers for teaching and learning, and distance education units.

CONTENTS

Chapter 1, "The New Economy Meets the Ivory Tower," is an introduction to the major trends and issues in higher education leading to the need for faculty development in the use of technology. Some of the greatest challenges faced by institutions are set forth, such as planning and budgeting for instructional technology, designing appropriate organizational structures and communication tools, and faculty incentives and rewards. Finally, some of the best practices, discoveries, and experiments found in the benchmarking study are previewed.

In Chapter 2, "Benchmarking Best Practices in Faculty Instructional Development," the authors present the methodology used in the benchmarking study and discuss its application in higher education and the corporate sector. The steps we took to identify and examine the "best practice" institutions are outlined in some detail.

The remaining chapters, which contain case studies from each of the "best practice" institutions, form the heart of the book. The University of Central Florida case (Chapter 3) provides an overview of faculty development initiatives, including an online course that prepares faculty to teach online. Collège Boréal (Chapter 4) is a case study in institutional "immersion" in technology and the challenges of putting pedagogy first. Virginia Tech (Chapter 5) has received national attention for numerous instructional technology innovations, such as the Math Emporium, but the drivers of change for faculty had been in place since 1993 through the Faculty Development Institute. Bellevue Community College (Chapter 6) offers many support programs for faculty teaching with technology, and this case study recounts the various initiatives and strategic vision. Finally, California State University's Center for Distributed Learning (Chapter 7) is an incubator for cutting-edge instructional innovations that have reached far beyond California.

Although the chapters vary greatly in substance, they generally adhere to the following structure: institutional setting, technology infrastructure, organizational infrastructure, major instructional technology initiatives, approach to faculty development, incentives for faculty participation, impact on teaching and learning, lessons learned, and future directions. Chapter 8, "Beyond Button-Pushing: Using Technology to Improve Learning," concludes the book with a discussion of the overall findings from the study, drawn from both the preliminary "screening" phase and the institutional site visits. The enthusiasm, idealism, and commitment to teaching and learning displayed at each institution are underscored as common themes and perhaps the key to each institution's success.

ACKNOWLEDGMENTS

The study on which this book is based is itself a model of collaboration. Many people gave freely of their time and resources to make this project succeed. We would especially like to thank and acknowledge the "best practice" institutions for hosting our site visits and letting us share your stories with the larger higher education community. These institutions include University of Central Florida, Collège Boréal, Virginia Tech, Bellevue Community College, and the California State University Center for Distributed Learning. In particular, we are most grateful to the 14 talented individuals from these institutions that contributed chapters to this book. We recognize the difficulty and commitment it has taken to develop your award-winning programs, let alone write about them.

Special thanks go to our friend and colleague Jim Mingle, who provided leadership and expertise throughout the benchmarking study and subsequently inspired the idea for this book. It was his suggestion that encouraged us to take on this task and disseminate the faculty development experiences of these institutions more widely. We also thank Dr. Jim Davis from the University of Denver who gave us early advice in choosing a publisher, which resulted in our connection with Oryx Press.

Finally, much of the credit for this book goes to the staff at the American Productivity & Quality Center (APQC). In particular, we are indebted to Marisa Brown and Kimberly Lopez for their extraordinary work in organizing and managing the benchmarking study. We should note, however, that the conclusions we draw in this book represent our own opinions, not necessarily those of APQC, the study report, or the institutions represented herein.

Rhonda M. Epper
A. W. (Tony) Bates

CHAPTER 1

The New Economy Meets the Ivory Tower

Rhonda M. Epper

sk most college faculty members about teaching with technology and you are likely to hear both fear and excitement—fear that they may lack the expertise and institutional support to use the new tools, and excitement about the possibilities of improving the way they teach and their students learn. Until recently, college teaching innovations were relatively few and far between. For literally centuries, professors needed only themselves and a place to lecture to carry out the educational mission. There were no instructional designers, Web programmers, computer graphics experts, or project managers throughout most of the history of higher education. Faculty work was basically a solitary pursuit. Now it is likely to be a group activity involving a wide range of professionals from both inside and outside the institution.

To cope with and take advantage of the technological and pedagogical shifts occurring in the teaching profession, faculty need new kinds of expertise and skill not required in the past. If institutions expect faculty to embrace these changes, then institutions must tackle the difficult task of providing faculty with the resources and support structures necessary to carry out today's educational mission.

In 1998, the American Productivity & Quality Center (APQC) and the State Higher Education Executive Officers (SHEEO), along with 45 postsecondary institutions and corporations across North America, conducted a benchmarking study on faculty development in the use of technology.[1] The purpose of the project was to locate and study organizations that were doing an exemplary job of teaching faculty how to use technology more effectively in their courses. The findings of the study included a set of "best practices" and strategies for allowing institutional leaders to build programs that support effective integration of technology into instruction.

This chapter first sets out the major trends and issues in higher education that led to the benchmarking study, explains the major institutional challenges to supporting faculty use of technology in teaching, and previews some of the best practices, discoveries, and experiments found in the benchmarking study and described in later chapters.

TRENDS AND ISSUES UNDERLYING THE NEED FOR FACULTY INSTRUCTIONAL DEVELOPMENT

The most significant changes in higher education often happen as a result of pressures outside the academy. While the "information revolution" has already transformed, eliminated, and created industries throughout the world, it has only scratched the surface of higher education. Several trends are putting pressure on higher education leaders to help prepare their campuses and their faculty to fully implement new instructional technologies. These trends include (1) the rise of economic and social forces promoting the use of technology in all aspects of society; (2) the need for more flexible approaches to teaching and learning; (3) the new competitive landscape in higher education; and (4) technology's potential to improve the quality of teaching and learning.

Economic and Social Forces Promoting the Use of Technology in All Aspects of Society

Technology has had a tremendous influence on our work and personal lives. Computers have become so embedded in the ways we work and communicate that we scarcely notice the remarkable technological advances and the speed at which these changes are occurring. A few statistics will illustrate the ever-expanding reach of technology: By the end of 2000, the number of people with Internet access reached over 300 million worldwide (up nearly 80% from 1999). The amount of information available online increased tenfold between 1997 and 2000 to more than a billion discrete Web pages.[2] Furthermore, our use of the Internet is expanding to include everyday activities, such as shopping. In January 2001, the U.S. Department of Commerce's Government Working Group on Electronic Commerce estimated "business to consumer" e-commerce transactions at over $60 billion in 2000 with a prediction of up to $144 billion by 2003. "Business to business" e-commerce transactions were estimated to exceed $184 billion in 2000, growing to between $634 billion and

$3.9 trillion by 2003. The report predicts that by 2003, some 80% of all business-to-business transactions could occur online.[3]

The U.S. economy grew markedly during the past decade, driven by the powerful combination of rapid technological innovation, sharply falling computer and technology prices, and "booming investment in IT goods and services across virtually all American industries."[4] Such investments and productivity gains have produced dramatic shifts in today's workforce composition. Although the economy has slowed significantly in 2001, the transformations of the past decade have produced a new economy powered not only by technology, but by the continuous advancement and application of human knowledge.

A few years ago, Peter Drucker wrote an article for the *Atlantic Monthly* entitled "The Age of Social Transformation" in which he described the rise of the "Knowledge Worker" (a term he coined in 1959) and its impact on society. According to Drucker, the new knowledge-based society—brought about chiefly through technological advances—has created the first society in history in which ordinary people "do not earn their daily bread by the sweat of their brow," and "honest work does not mean a callused hand." In contrast to workers of the Industrial Age, knowledge workers gain access to jobs and social position through their formal and informal educational experiences. Knowledge is something you can carry with you from employer to employer, and serves as a ticket to greater economic prosperity. Moreover, in a knowledge-based economy, the workers own the means of production that drive the economy. Thus, knowledge acquisition (i.e., education), technological advancement, and economic success are closely interrelated—a point not lost on the majority of Americans, who believe that colleges are teaching students important things and that higher education is more important than ever as a key to a middle-class lifestyle.

The Need for More Flexible Approaches to Teaching and Learning

Higher education has been touched by the seismic shifts technology has brought to our global economy and society. Perhaps most significantly, the marketplace of higher education is now exposed to intense competitive pressures defined largely by consumer needs and desires and changing workforce demands. Although many people within the academy still resist the idea of a "market" mentality in higher education with colleges pandering to students and commercial interests, these voices grow fainter as more faculty and administrators embrace the opportunities of "anytime, anyplace" teaching and learning.

While video-based "distance learning" grew steadily throughout the 1980s and 1990s, such learning was sufficiently separated from the core of the academic enterprise to be nonthreatening and mostly a non-issue. But the emergence of the Internet, e-mail, and the World Wide Web brought new meaning and power to "distance learning." Two surveys conducted by NCES in 1995 and 1998 demonstrate this point. Among all higher education institutions offering any distance education, the percentages of institutions using two-way interactive video and one-way prerecorded video were essentially the same in 1998 as in 1995. However, the percentage of institutions using asynchronous Internet-based technologies nearly tripled from 22% of institutions in 1995 to 60% in 1998.[5]

The NCES surveys further showed that student enrollment in college-level, credit-granting distance education courses nearly doubled from 753,640 in 1994–1995 to 1,343,580 in 1997–1998. At the same time, the number of courses offered in this mode nearly doubled (25,730 to 47,540) while the number of degree and certificate programs offered also nearly doubled (690 to 1,190). The attractiveness of this delivery mode is also illustrated by the percentage of higher education institutions offering distance education courses, which increased by about one-third, from 33% in 1994–1995 to 44% in 1997–1998. And these statistics represent only distance education in which some form of technology is used as the *primary* mode of delivery; no industry estimates or data sources capture the number of faculty or courses using technology or Web-based resources as *part* of their course delivery. The number of hybrid or partially Web-based courses is likely much larger than fully Web-based courses and will probably increase as mainstream faculty become more comfortable using technology in instruction. As a result, most students engaged in online learning today are the institution's own resident (and increasingly computer savvy) students who choose to supplement their course load with online offerings as a matter of convenience or preference. While much rhetoric and policy revolves around a "global" academic marketplace, the largest market for distance learning may actually be local.

The New Competitive Landscape in Higher Education

Traditional higher education institutions are certainly not the only players in the new market for higher education. Technology has lowered the entry barriers for new providers of postsecondary education because of its low cost compared to traditional "bricks and mortar" institutions.[6] Both for-profit companies and aggressive continuing education units of public and private universities are moving quickly to serve the growing market for "lifelong learning" among employed adults. Institutions like the University of Phoenix and National Technological University (NTU) have successfully served this population for years. Phoenix's for-profit parent company, The Apollo Group, has also enjoyed remarkable success on Wall Street. While traditional higher education institutions have scoffed at Phoenix's blatant profit motives, a number of them have also taken steps to emulate the institution's success. NTU now operates a for-profit subsidiary created to help alleviate the financial challenges of expanding and upgrading the institution's technology and to better market its services.[7]

Even some of the world's most elite colleges and universities are creating or entering into agreements with for-profit entities that can help market and sell their online course offerings. Cornell University, the University of Maryland, and Columbia University have created for-profit subsidiaries to develop, market, and manage their distance education programs.[8] Unext.com, a well-financed online learning venture, is partnering with prestigious institutions to supply its educational content. In the spring of 2001, these partners included Carnegie Mellon, Columbia, Stanford, the University of Chicago, and the London School of Economics and Political Science. Another online education company, NextEd, is partnering with at least nine universities on four continents to deliver graduate and professional courses online in Asia. Among the participants in NextEd's Global Education Alliance are Athabasca University, Rochester Institute of Technology, University of South Australia, Auckland University of Technology, and Chung Yuan Christian University in Taiwan.[9] Universitas 21 is another international educational venture that is attempting to capture a share of the growing market for online education.[10] Fathom.com and Global Education Network are among many others on the rapidly growing list of "new providers" of educational content.

But for all the news coverage, investor frenzy, and investor fallout, the majority of online courses today are still being offered by traditional nonprofit colleges and universities. Carol Twigg argues that only a handful of truly significant "new providers" are delivering courses to large numbers of students: "The vast majority of for-credit online and distance learning going on today is being conducted by highly traditional colleges and universities, building on well-established academic structures and conditions for successful learning. These initiatives create greater opportunities for students as well as greater competitive pressures among established institutions, but it's a stretch to call the universities of Maryland, Indiana and Wisconsin, for example, 'new providers.'"[11]

What may be surprising to some is that the idea of universities having financial ties to corporations and profit-based interests is not new. Universities have been earning royalties from campus-based inventions since the Bayh–Dole Act of 1980 first allowed them to patent the results of federally funded research, and license their inventions to U.S. companies.[12] What is new is the initiative institutions are taking to move beyond their research parks and tap into the burgeoning market for online *courses*, which can be packaged and sold over the Internet. But fundamental issues of ownership and copyright are still unresolved on most campuses and most faculty are not at all sure their interests are being served in the new marketplace.

Technology's Potential to Improve the Quality of Teaching and Learning

Besides having to respond to new market pressures, college leaders and faculty are realizing that the intelligent use of technology can really improve the quality of teaching. Undoubtedly some faculty members cling nervously to their tested and trusted pedagogies whenever new learning technologies are presented, but these faculty are increasingly in the minority. The most recent national faculty survey from UCLA's Higher Education Research Institute reports that a full 87% of faculty believe that student use of computers *enhances* student learning.[13] Considering that most discussion about evaluation and effectiveness of technology revolves around the "no significant difference" phenomenon,[14] it is somewhat surprising to see a large majority of faculty express such confidence in technology's potential to actually enhance the learning process.

My co-editor of this book, Tony Bates, argues in his latest book that comparing the relative effectiveness of technology-based teaching with traditional face-to-face teaching is a futile effort. The results of such comparisons (i.e., no significant difference) are already known. More often, he states, different or new learning outcomes can be achieved through the use of technology that need not imitate the goals and assumptions of classroom teaching.[15] So, what exactly are the "new learning outcomes" that technology is better able to impart to students? It may be that the new learning outcomes are not so new at all, but, in fact, different from those of the traditional classroom.

In 1987, well before the ascendance of technology in mainstream instruction, Art Chikering and Zelda Gamson published "Seven Principles of Good Practice in Undergraduate Education."[16] The seven principles suggest that good instructional practice:

- Encourages contact between students and faculty.
- Develops reciprocity and cooperation among students.
- Uses active learning techniques.
- Gives prompt feedback.
- Emphasizes time-on-task.
- Communicates high expectations.
- Respects diverse talents and ways of learning.

Interestingly, these principles were designed during the peak of a national focus on "undergraduate reform" and calls from political leaders for "quality improvement" in undergraduate education. The seven principles were used to critique, guide, and serve as a model against the predominant form of learning in undergraduate education, namely, the passive lecture–discussion format. The lecture format, according to Guskin, Shulman, and others, is contrary to almost every optimal setting for student learning.[17]

Although the seven principles were not designed to be an endorsement of technology-based teaching, technology in many ways facilitates the use of these effective instructional practices. For example, "active" learning implies that students learn best by "doing" or directly engaging in the application of content, not just by listening to teachers talk about it. Students need to talk and write about what they are learning and relate it to their past experiences to "internalize" new concepts. A wide range of instructional technologies encourages powerful "interactive" learning settings where students gain a deeper understanding of process and content. Computer simulation software allows students to experiment with and manipulate variables and instantly see the resulting changes. Sometimes computer-based experiments simulate events that are impossible to replicate in a real-life or laboratory-based experiment. An example of such an experiment is a simulation developed at California State University that traces biological evolution (over millions of years) under conditions set up and manipulated by the student.

Using technology for interactive learning truly takes advantage of technology's potential to change education. Some observers argue that technology should be used to make "information delivery" more efficient, thus giving faculty members more time to work directly with students.[18] Although more efficient content delivery is certainly an attractive and useful purpose of technology, it stops far short of realizing the ultimate benefit for students. As stated recently by a professor of interdisciplinary humanities at Arizona State University:

> Instructional technologies should not be used as elaborate versions of portable student slates, larger and dynamic blackboards, overhead projectors or textbooks. These are static technologies, used traditionally to make information available to large amounts of students. . . . In essence every classroom should be a knowledge laboratory using management strategies and complex knowledge matrices that require students to test and apply that knowledge in simulated applications.[19]

Besides facilitating active learning, other compelling elements of good practice are seen in technology's simple but powerful tools for communicating between and among faculty and students. Many faculty who teach online courses or use e-mail to communicate with students report a much higher level of interaction than they experienced in the past. Most people think of the online learning experience as being cold, impersonal, and disconnected from the intimacy of a live classroom, but students and faculty report the opposite. A professor in the humanities recently described his online teaching experience at the 2000 American Historical Association Annual Conference:

> Early in my on-line teaching I was asked what were the demographics of the class. I had to laugh because I had no idea how old my students were, their age, race, appearance or even, in some cases, their gender.

I was at the same time teaching a live class on the same subject. Those students I knew by sight. I could have estimated their average age and so on. But I did not know the students in my live class as individuals. My only contact with them were a few moments once a week when they might speak up in class, and their exams. In the on-line class, on the other hand, I could say in some detail what sort of students those people were. I could tell which ones understood how to do research and how to do evidence. I knew which ones had a religious prejudice, which ones tended to reductionism, and so on. In short, I knew my virtual students far better than I knew my live students.[20]

When students describe their learning experiences online, they acknowledge greater levels of interaction, but some still prefer a certain level of face-to-face contact with their professor and other students. The University of Central Florida (UCF) found this to be the case for students after conducting extensive evaluation studies of their online course offerings. Consequently, UCF has placed a greater emphasis on helping faculty create "partial" Web-based courses that still require some face-to-face contact.

The rapid advancement of information technology into all aspects of personal and work life is hitting home for many faculty members. It has created a sense of excitement around the reexamination of pedagogy and a renewed interest in exploring new realms of education. The next section will explain how some of the excitement faculty are experiencing is accompanied by anxiety and uncertainty, and how campuses are responding to these concerns.

INSTITUTIONAL CHALLENGES IN SUPPORTING FACULTY USE OF TECHNOLOGY IN INSTRUCTION

For several legitimate reasons, most faculty have at least some doubts and concerns about incorporating technology into their teaching. The 1999 UCLA national faculty survey found that "keeping up with information technology" was a significant source of stress for 67% of college faculty during the past two years. This technology-related stress outranked traditional stress producers for faculty such as research and publishing demands, teaching load, and the review and promotion process.[21] Change is never easy—it takes time, involves risk and hard work—but it can be made easier with appropriate planning, support, and incentives. Colleges and universities have struggled on all three fronts in their efforts to encourage faculty to use technology in instruction. While some institutions are making real advances in faculty development, others are constrained by a lack of money or commitment.

In the 2000 national Campus Computing survey, respondents cited "assisting faculty efforts to integrate technology into instruction" as the single most important technology challenge facing American colleges and universities over the next two to three years.[22] Institutional leaders evidently recognize the faculty development challenges before them. Yet *understanding* the critical need to put adequate resources, reliable infrastructure, and support systems in place is only the first step. College leaders must overcome some significant obstacles in creating an environment that *enables* faculty to make the best use of technology resources. Three major obstacles include the need for appropriate (1) planning and budgeting for instructional technology, (2) organizational structures and communication, and (3) faculty rewards and incentives.

Planning and Budgeting for Instructional Technology

One of the important lessons learned over the past decade in higher education is that while technology is obviously expensive, supporting its use is even more expensive. For the most part, state-level and campus leaders have been slow to realize that budgeting for the full costs associated with technology requires a sustained commitment, not just one-time funding for hardware acquisition. Support services, training, and replacement costs turn out to be larger than the initial investment, and therefore must be part of the ongoing planning and budgeting process. The early hope among state-level officials that technology would reduce the overall cost of higher education is not likely to be the case, even if per-unit costs decline with greater enrollments. Higher education institutions may, in fact, become more productive as a result of technology enhancements; but the large investments in infrastructure, equipment, support, and periodic replacement diminish the hope that it will cost the public or the individual less money.[23]

Even with their sizable investments in technology, Kenneth C. Green argues that colleges and universities underfund both the operating and infrastructure costs of technology for several reasons: the absence of a strategic or financial plan for technology, the inability to amortize, a reluctance to lease, the underpayment of technology support personnel, and a tendency to use technology well beyond its useful life.[24] The first of these, that is, lack of a strong strategic plan, severely inhibits widespread adoption and use of technology in instruction. If faculty are expected to implement technology in their courses, institutions must provide a supporting environment that enables them to do so successfully. One of the important findings of the APQC/SHEEO benchmarking study on faculty development was that institutions with the strongest programs to support faculty use of technology also had an overall campus culture pervaded by technology. This culture was typically supported by a range of strategies, which included:

- A strong strategic plan in which the use of technology for teaching plays a prominent role.
- Extensive investment in technology infrastructure.

- Support from senior leadership for the use of technology in teaching.
- Support for faculty members (e.g., training, technical support, project funding, release time, equipment).
- Support for students through computer access, Internet accounts, and financial support.

While each of these approaches individually helps to create a positive environment for faculty, their *combination* results in a culture that is "totally immersed" in teaching and learning with technology. Developing such a culture requires setting priorities, making new investments, and reallocating resources from lower to higher priorities. As noted by Bates (2000), "In the end, if teaching with technology is to be a key component of the institution, then the institution has to build it into its base operating budget."[25] This can be extremely difficult as teaching with technology becomes more popular among faculty. With more faculty using technology, some institutions (especially smaller ones) find they are unable to respond to the growing faculty demands for equipment, training, and support.

Organizational Structures and Communication

Most of the institutions examined in the APQC/SHEEO benchmarking study were characterized by both centralized and decentralized services to support faculty integration of technology in teaching. Centralized services included centers for faculty development, centers for teaching and learning, centers for instructional innovation, and the like. Some campuses also had a center for "distributed learning" that specifically supported faculty development of online teaching. An institution-wide center for faculty development (usually located within academic affairs) often operated alongside an institution-wide center for distributed learning (usually within the information technology reporting structure). A faculty development center typically supports the improvement of teaching in general, not just technology-based teaching. Centers for distributed learning focus on preparing faculty to offer Web-based instruction, and usually have one or more specialists in instructional design, Web programming, and graphics design.

Most faculty prefer to have technical support delivered "just-in-time" when and where they need it. As a result, a number of individual academic units (e.g., colleges or even large departments) employ a technical support person who can work one-on-one with faculty as needed. Decentralized services are often delivered alongside multiple centralized services within an institution. Although the activities may be somewhat coordinated, they are mostly duplicated and sometimes the support units themselves become competitive. This situation leads to confusion for faculty members on where they should go for help when they want to implement technology in their courses. In a recent

survey, the University of Michigan polled its faculty on which support resources they are most likely to use when they need help with instructional
technology. Thirteen different support units were listed with the majority of
respondents not even aware that many of them were available (see
Figure 1.1).[26]

The University of Michigan example is not used to argue for more or less
centralization in faculty support. Rather, it underscores the need for greater
coordination among support units, and clear and effective communication
channels on what resources are available to faculty. There is also a need for
greater coordination *across* institutions, especially within multicampus systems

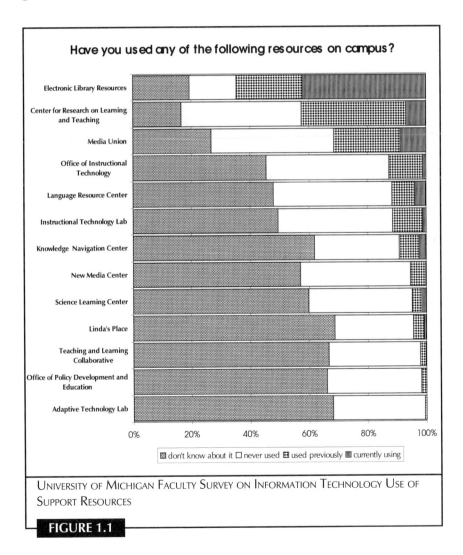

UNIVERSITY OF MICHIGAN FACULTY SURVEY ON INFORMATION TECHNOLOGY USE OF
SUPPORT RESOURCES

FIGURE 1.1

of higher education. The University of Wisconsin System has established a "Web-based Learning System Utility," which is used to support four of the major courseware programs in each of the 15 institutions and 26 campuses within the system. Blackboard, WebCT, Lotus Learning Space, and Prometheus are funded centrally. Hosting and faculty support for each of these programs is provided by one designated campus for all faculty within the system. Wisconsin officials report that this arrangement has proved effective in facilitating the use of Web-based instructional technology around the system, without dictating a single vendor for all faculty.

Faculty Rewards and Incentives

Another important challenge institutions face in creating an "enabling" environment for faculty use of instructional technology is the reward system. Both the formal reward structure and the general faculty ethos toward instructional innovation and experimentation have major effects on faculty behavior. In a recent review of the quality of undergraduate teaching and learning in the United States, George Kuh examined student experience in the 1990s with three of the most widely recognized processes that promote student learning: faculty–student interaction, peer cooperation, and active learning. In most institutions, save small colleges, the trends were toward less faculty–student interaction and less active learning.[27] A major reason cited in the study for this trend was faculty disengagement from their teaching interests and growing concern for their research and scholarly interests. This news is no surprise to the higher education community or to the public at large. However, there are legitimate and logical reasons for faculty to pursue excellence in research at the expense of excellence in teaching. Fundamentally, the reward system is at the heart of the problem.

The prevailing faculty reward system, which rewards active and productive researchers, not teachers, appears to be stronger than ever. This occurs despite at least a decade of internal reexamination of faculty roles and rewards[28] and external calls for change. Beginning in the mid-1980s, a combination of resource constraints and public scrutiny over the quality of undergraduate teaching caused many critics and public officials to began asking tough questions about the nature of faculty work. Studies of faculty workload and even mandates for change were issued from state legislatures and coordinating agencies across the United States.[29] Although these external pressures may have stimulated internal discussions of change, they have for the most part had little effect on the faculty reward structure.

"The condition of teaching is, in short, a pattern of contradictions,"[30] according to the late Ernie Boyer, who made probably the most well-known and prolific argument for a new definition of recognized scholarly activity in his

1990 *Scholarship Reconsidered*.[31] Many faculty members would prefer to spend time improving their teaching methodologies and working as a community, yet the values and traditions enforced by the reward system force them to focus on research productivity, often in a competitive and individualistic way.

Yet there is hope for change. Having greater impact than any attempt so far by legislators or faculty themselves to examine the nature of teaching and learning has been the availability and use of new technology. Regardless of what faculty believe about the ability of technology to improve teaching, its presence has sparked the most thorough self-examination of teaching and learning in recent history. There are a great many faculty members who are truly energized by the opportunities technology brings to teaching. Some faculty who have never engaged themselves in matters of pedagogy have been "set on fire" (in the words of a university academic officer) by working with technology-enhanced teaching tools. In many cases faculty become inspired by their students' enthusiasm for and considerable expertise in the use of technology.

There are also a great many faculty who fear the changes to traditional faculty roles that are inevitable in technology-based and student-centered learning environments. Alongside these fears are concerns (even among technology supporters) about intellectual property and copyright of materials created in whole or in part by faculty. This is an area in which almost every institution is struggling to sort out who's entitled to what share of ownership in the development of technology-based learning materials. There are no simple or ideal solutions to this very complex issue, but faculty and institutions are making progress. Some institutions have posted their intellectual property policies and other helpful information on Web sites. For example, MIT lists a comparison of its policy with peer institutions' policies (http://web.mit.edu/committees/ip/policies.html). The University of Texas System has posted its intellectual property policy on the Web, including a version "In Plain English," which is relatively easy to understand (http://www.utsystem.edu/ogc/intellectualproperty/ippol.htm). For a full discussion of intellectual property, copyright, and revenue generation in higher education, see Tony Bates's (2000) *Managing Technological Change* and Carol Twigg's "Who Owns Online Courses and Course Materials?"[32]

BEST PRACTICES, EXPERIMENTS, DISCOVERIES

The challenges previously set forth may seem daunting, but they are not insurmountable. Higher education institutions across the United States and around the world are putting a great deal of resources and creativity into helping faculty use instructional technology. In addition, there are a growing number of "how-to" guides to online teaching being published in both print and electronic formats. For example, the League for Innovation in the Community College published a *Faculty Guide for Moving Teaching and Learning to the Web* in 1999.[33] McGraw-Hill published *You Can Teach Online* in 2001, which includes a companion Web site.[34] Some institutions and private companies offer online "courses" to help faculty learn about teaching online. Penn State, for example, created a resource guide on the Web called Faculty Development 101.[35] The Web page is not a structured course, but gives advice to faculty on such things as leading interactive discussions online. The University of Maryland University College developed a site called Virtual Resource Site for Teaching with Technology (http://www.umuc.edu/virtualteaching/) for instructors not only in Maryland, but anywhere. The site contains examples of assignments or exercises that are used in online courses at various institutions.[36] In addition, a number of private companies are convinced that there is a market demand for resources to help faculty prepare to teach online. University Access (now Quisic) and OnlineLearning.net are two examples of companies that offer "courses" on how to teach in a Web-based environment. There are also companies that offer a full range of services—from course management software to Web hosting to faculty development—in partnership with institutions as they implement online courses and programs. Eduprise, WebCT, Blackboard, and eCollege.com are among the most prominent players in this highly competitive industry.

Most of the creative work, however, on finding solutions to meet faculty needs is happening within institutions of higher education. As identified initially in the APQC/SHEEO benchmarking study, some of the most innovative approaches to faculty development are contained in the chapters that follow. The University of Central Florida, Collège Boréal, Virginia Tech, Bellevue Community College, and the California State University Center for Distributed Learning represent a diverse set of institutions, all of which have successfully experimented with new solutions for helping faculty incorporate technology into instruction.

The University of Central Florida (UCF) has put in place orientations and faculty development programs to assist faculty from the day they join the institution. Many of the programs are designed to meet the individual learning needs of faculty, while being scalable for institution-wide use. A hallmark of UCF's faculty development initiatives is their nationally recognized online course designed to help faculty prepare to teach in an online environment. Known as IDL6543, the course combines face-to-face class meetings, hands-on labs, online modules, consultations with instructional designers, and homework activities. The IDL6543 course helps faculty develop one module of the course they plan to deliver online. In addition to the face-to-face consultations and classes available for faculty to learn, programs are being developed as just-in-time training or self-paced study available anytime, anywhere.

Collège Boréal, in Ontario, Canada, operates a faculty resource center called *La Cuisine* (literally translated as "The Kitchen"). It serves as a place where faculty can gather to develop and share new skills and approaches to facilitate the integration of various technologies into the learning process. *La Cuisine* provides access to a variety of multimedia tools, and is staffed by a full-time coordinator/instructional designer. Responsibilities of *La Cuisine* staff include one-on-one training sessions with faculty, organizing and offering various workshops focusing on educational aspects of technology, and researching the various trends and resources available in other institutions. Collège Boréal also offers decentralized support for faculty through their "Resource Person" model. Four full-time faculty members work as resource persons, one in each of the college's four schools: Technology and Natural Sciences, Business and Office Administration, Health Sciences, and Human Sciences. These faculty are relieved of their teaching duties in order to assist their colleagues in their instructional development initiatives. They handle much of the troubleshooting for less experienced faculty and guide course material development projects in cooperation with *La Cuisine*.

Virginia Tech, a pioneer institution in the use of instructional technologies, established a Faculty Development Institute (FDI) in 1993. The FDI assists faculty in learning how to use technology in teaching, and has served almost 100% of the faculty. As the FDI has evolved over the years, it has been informed by three compelling questions: (1) how faculty can best use instructional technology to improve their teaching; (2) what the impact of this technology is on student learning that occurs in various settings and under many conditions; and (3) how the interaction between faculty and students will drive discovery. The FDI is designed as a four-year recurring program that will help all Virginia Tech faculty members learn how to integrate technology into their instruction through an intensive workshop environment. One of the incentives for faculty to attend FDI is a new desktop computer, an Ethernet/Internet connection, a standardized package of software, and ongoing support. The FDI is also used as a way to establish an equipment and software replacement cycle for faculty.

Bellevue Community College (BCC) encourages faculty development in a number of ways, including resource allocations designated for professional development, individual grants to faculty to develop online materials, released time, and a Faculty Resource Center, which operates in conjunction with an NSF-funded program called the NorthWest Center for Emerging Technology (NWCET). The NWCET develops curriculum standards for information technology careers with other colleges in the region. Staff positions within the Faculty Resource Center are funded both by the NWCET and BCC, and are assisted by student interns. The resource center provides faculty with not only technical assistance, but also curriculum design. It offers regular workshops on creating and implementing online courses, and a Web-based tutorial for placing materials on the Internet.

The California State University's (CSU) Center for Distributed Learning is a systemwide resource designed to assist faculty and academic technology staff members in creating, identifying, and using multimedia learning materials effectively. One of its central and most innovative projects is MERLOT (Multimedia Education Resource for Learning and Online Teaching). MERLOT (www.merlot.org) is an open source collection of over 4,000 Web-based teaching and learning materials. These materials are interactive modules, simulations, tutorials, and other course material that faculty can integrate into their own curriculum and pedagogy. It is a searchable database organized by discipline or subject. Materials indexed on the site may contain peer reviews, learning assignments, user comments, technical tips, and IMS metadata. In addition, MERLOT supports faculty development programs to assist faculty integration of Web-based materials into their teaching.

MERLOT offers a solution to the many obstacles faced by faculty who want to use the Internet in their teaching. Among the most stubborn obstacles are difficulty finding relevant digital materials, evaluating the quality of materials once found, and integrating the materials into a pedagogical context that meets the learning needs of students. These problems are not unique to faculty in the California State University System. University systems across North America have recognized the power and usefulness of MERLOT and its faculty development processes, and have joined forces with CSU to scale the project up to a national and even international level. For the 2000–2001 fiscal year, 23 university systems, individual institutions, and private college consortia joined the MERLOT project and dedicated both financial and human resources to making MERLOT tools and processes available to their faculty.

With all the creative work going on in the world of Internet-based teaching and learning, and the rate at which new discoveries and improvements occur, it is hard to say that the group of institutions represented in this book is the singular "best" of "best practices." Without a doubt there are pockets of innovation and great things happening at many institutions throughout the world. However, I can say with certainty that these institutions are *among* the best and most innovative in the field. Their stories of challenges, failures, and successes along the way are worth telling, and will serve as useful blueprints for others who are on the path to change.

NOTES

1. American Productivity & Quality Center and State Higher Education Executive Officers, *Today's Teaching and Learning: Leveraging Technology: Results from the Faculty Instructional Development Study* (Houston, TX: American Productivity & Quality Center, 1999).

2. Inktomi Corporation and NEC Research Institute, January 2000. www.inktomi.com/webmap.

3. U.S. Government Working Group on Electronic Commerce, "Leadership for the New Millennium: Delivering on Digital Progress and Prosperity" (Washington, DC: U.S. Department of Commerce, January 2001).

4. U.S. Department of Commerce, "Digital Economy 2000" (Washington, DC: Economics and Statistics Administration, Office of Policy Development, U.S. Department of Commerce, June 2000).

5. U.S. Department of Education, National Center for Education Statistics, Postsecondary Education Quick Information System, Survey on Distance Education Courses Offered by Higher Education Institutions, 1995, and Survey on Distance Education at Postsecondary Education Institutions, 1998–1999.

6. James R. Mingle. "Responding to the New Market for Higher Education," *AGB Priorities*, 11 (Summer 1998). Washington, DC: Association of Governing Boards.

7. Daniel Gross. "Not for Profit? Not Exactly," *University Business*, 2, No. 3 (April 1999): 31–36.

8. Sarah Carr. "A For-Profit Subsidiary Will Market Cornell's Distance Programs," *Chronicle of Higher Education* (March 14, 2000).

9. Geoffrey Maslen. "Nine Universities Collaborate on Online Instruction in Asia." *Chronicle of Higher Education* (June 30, 2000): A43.

10. Geoffrey Maslin. "Rupert Murdoch Joins with 18 Universities in Distance Education Venture." *Chronicle of Higher Education* (May 17, 2000).

11. Carol A. Twigg. "All the Wrong Places," *The Learning MarketSpace* (January 1, 2000). (www.center.rpi.edu/Lforum/LdfLM.html).

12. Eyal Press, and Jennifer Washburn. "The Kept University," *The Atlantic Monthly*, 285 (March 2000): 39-54.

13. Linda J. Sax, Alexander W. Astin, William S. Korn, and Shannon K. Gilmartin. "The American College Teacher: National Norms for the 1998-99 HERI Faculty Survey" (Los Angeles: Higher Education Research Institute, Graduate School of Education & Information Studies, University of California, Los Angeles, September 1999).

14. Thomas Russell. *The No Significant Difference Phenomenon* (Raleigh: North Carolina State University Office of Instructional Telecommunications, 1999).

15. A. W. Bates. *Managing Technological Change: Strategies for College and University Leaders* (San Francisco: Jossey-Bass, 2000).

16. Arthur W. Chickering, and Zelda Gamson. "Seven Principles for Good Practice in Undergraduate Education," *AAHE Bulletin* (March 1987). Washington, DC: American Association for Higher Education.

17. Alan E. Guskin. "Restructuring the Role of Faculty," *Change Magazine* (September/October 1999). Washington, DC: American Association for Higher Education and Heldref Publications.

18. Ibid.

19. Paul Michael Privateer. "Academic Technology and the Future of Higher Education," *The Journal of Higher Education*, 70, No. 1 (January/February 1999): 60–79.

20. E. L. Skip Knox. "The Rewards of Teaching Online." Presentation delivered at the Annual Conference of the American Historical Association, Chicago: January 6–9, 2000.

21. Linda J. Sax, Alexander W. Astin, William S. Korn, and Shannon K. Gilmartin. "The American College Teacher: National Norms for the 1998–99 HERI Faculty Survey" (Los Angeles: Higher Education Research Institute, Graduate School of Education & Information Studies, University of California, Los Angeles, September 1999).

22. Kenneth C. Green. *The 2000 National Survey of Information Technology in Higher Education* (Encino, CA: The Campus Computing Project, 2000).

23. Margaret A. Miller, and Steven W. Gilbert. "Educational Uses of Information Technology: A View for State Leaders," *Transforming Postsecondary Education for the 21st Century: Briefing Papers* (Denver, CO: Education Commission of the States, 1999).

24. Kenneth C. Green. "What is Information Technology in Higher Education?" Working Paper prepared for the *Executive Forum on Managing the Costs of IT in Higher Education*, sponsored by Seton Hall University, Princeton, NJ: April 15-17, 1999.

25. A. W. Bates. *Managing Technological Change: Strategies for College and University Leaders* (San Francisco: Jossey-Bass, 2000), p. 157.

26. University of Michigan Senate Advisory Committee on University Affairs and the Chief Information Officer, "Faculty Survey: Information Technology Uses, Resources and Support" (Ann Arbor: University of Michigan, August 1999).

27. George D. Kuh. "How Are We Doing? Tracking the Quality of the Undergraduate Experience, 1960s to the Present," *The Review of Higher Education*, 22, No. 2 (1999): 99–119.

28. Eugene Rice. "The Academic Professor in Transition: Toward a New Social Function," *Teaching Sociology*, 14 (1991): 12–23.

29. Alene Bycer Russell. *Faculty Workload: State and System Perspectives* (Denver, CO: State Higher Education Executive Officers and Education Commission of the States, 1992).

30. Earnest L. Boyer. *College: The Undergraduate Experience in America* (New York: Harper & Row, 1987).

31. Ernest L. Boyer. *Scholarship Reconsidered: Priorities of the Professoriate* (Princeton, NJ: Carnegie Foundation for the Advancement of Teaching, 1990).

32. Carol A. Twigg. "Who Owns Online Courses and Course Materials? Intellectual Property Policies for a New Learning Environment" (Troy, NY: Center for Academic Transformation, The Pew Learning and Technology Program, 2000).

33. Judith V. Boettcher, and Rita-Marie Conrad. *Faculty Guide for Moving Teaching and Learning to the Web* (Mission Viejo, CA: League for Innovation in the Community College, 1999).

34. Gary S. Moore, Kathryn Winograd, and Dan Lange. *You Can Teach Online: Building a Creative Learning Environment* (New York: McGraw-Hill Higher Education, 2001).

35. Dan Carnevale. "Instructors Take a Turn as Students to Learn about Online Teaching," *Chronicle of Higher Education* (February 18, 2000).

36. Jeffrey R. Young. "Web Site Provides Advice on Teaching With Technology," *Chronicle of Higher Education* (April 5, 2000).

CHAPTER 2

Benchmarking Best Practices in Faculty Instructional Development

Marisa Martin Brown and Ron Webb

The past decade has seen wrenching change for many organizations. As organizations have looked for ways to survive and remain profitable, a simple but powerful change strategy called "benchmarking" has evolved and become popular. Benchmarking can be described as a process by which organizations learn, modeled on the human learning process. A good working definition is "the process of identifying, learning, and adapting outstanding practices and processes from any organization, anywhere in the world, to help an organization improve its performance." The underlying rationale for benchmarking is that learning by example, from best-practice cases, is the most effective means of understanding the principles and the specifics of effective practices.

The most important aspect of benchmarking is that it does not use solutions to a problem prescribed by experts. Rather, it is a process through which participants learn about successful practices in other organizations and then draw on those cases to develop solutions that are most suitable for their own organizations. To understand the benchmarking study, in which the organizations in this book participated, it is important to distinguish between two related but distinct terms: "benchmarks" and "benchmarking." Benchmarking is the process of identifying, learning, adapting, and implementing outstanding practices and processes from organizations, both similar and dissimilar, to help an organization improve its performance. More simply stated—benchmarking is "finding and adapting best practices." Benchmarks are outcomes such as numbers, measures, and standards that identify the gaps between an institution and its peers. Both benchmarks and benchmarking are important, but they are not the same. Benchmarking can be seen as the continuation of the use of benchmarks. Benchmarking is the *process* used to achieve those benchmarks.

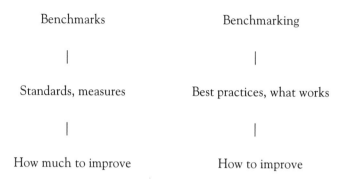

Benchmarks	Benchmarking
|	|
Standards, measures	Best practices, what works
|	|
How much to improve	How to improve

Benchmarking relies primarily on the use of what is termed "process benchmarking," where the focus is on finding best practices in a given process. For example, it is one thing to know that Institution A's improved admissions process saved it hundreds of thousands of dollars in decreased time and reduced paperwork, but it's another to know exactly how the organization achieved such a benchmark. This is process benchmarking—asking the who, what, when, where, why, and how questions behind the numbers.

Benchmarking is considered to be a major driver of organizational change. For example, once you have truly understood Institution A's faculty development process, you can determine if that process will "fit" within your organization. Sometimes these practices are transferable, but more often than not they must be adapted to each unique organization. If Institution A has trustees that will make a large up-front investment in the technology infrastructure needed to improve distance learning but Institution B has no funds to do so, then chances are Institution A's technology practices need to be extensively tailored to work for Institution B. Fortunately, just understanding another organization's processes and practices often is a great starting point for changing the status quo within your own organization. First, by identifying potentially inefficient, unnecessary, or exceptionally costly steps in your organizational processes, you can prioritize what you need to learn from other organizations. Second, by understanding how other organizations avoid or minimize the impact of those same (or similar) steps, you can reap the true rewards of benchmarking.

Interestingly, while benchmarking organizations from within the same business or government sector may lead to substantial improvements, benchmarking outside of one's own industry or discipline may result in some of the most revolutionary changes. Educators have historically looked to benchmark with other educators, and usually only with institutions like their own (e.g., research institutions with research institutions and liberal arts institutions with liberal arts institutions). In doing so, they may miss some of the most important breakthrough best practices from other sectors or industries. Initially business, government, and healthcare organizations also commonly believed they could learn best practices only from their own industry, and from organizations with the same characteristics—for example, size, culture, or location. However, benchmarking exercises have shown that organizations can learn effectively from organizations outside their sector, regardless of size, location, and so forth. Breakthrough benchmarking—the kind that results in dramatic improvement—most often comes from stepping away from your own organizational context and getting a fresh perspective.

One of the best instances of breakthrough benchmarking is the example of Delta Air Lines and its desire to service its aircraft more safely and efficiently.[1] In the airline business, most of the major players had similar processes for "turning around" an airplane (i.e., getting it ready for its next flight as soon as it lands). Looking outside the industry though, Delta identified a group of professionals who were *truly* world-class in servicing and refueling in a quick and safe manner: an Indianapolis 500 pit crew. Indy pit crews work in hazardous conditions with stringent turnaround requirements (pit crews are expected to change four tires and fill a gas tank in approximately 20 seconds). Based on information gathered through process benchmarking the pit crew's operations, Delta was able to significantly cut the amount of time it took to service its planes. Process improvements gleaned from the pit crew also enabled the company to improve the safety conditions for its workers.

As startling as this may sound, such breakthrough benchmarking has its place in the educational arena as well. One higher education consortium looking to improve its measurement of institutional performance outcomes benchmarked a company for whom successful performance of their products is critical: Raytheon TI Systems, a defense contractor. Another group of higher education institutions looking to find best practices in creating electronic student services benchmarked with a Canadian telephone company that provides customers the ability to control their phone service themselves by adding or changing the services on their own phone.

As a relatively new process improvement tool in education, there are some misconceptions about benchmarking. The following points clarify some common misunderstandings about benchmarking:

- It is not copying. Rarely can anyone take a best practice and directly copy it into their own organization. It must be adapted. The reality may be that only bits or pieces of a best practice are useful or adaptable to another organization.

- It is not spying. Benchmarking is conducted openly, with cooperation from and collaboration with the organization being studied.
- It is not scapegoating or blaming. It is about finding information for improvement.
- It is not just reading articles, case studies, or abstracts of best practices. These help, but written materials never completely describe how processes work in actual practice. Learning the tacit knowledge, culture, structure, and drivers of change takes personal involvement, conversation, observation, and interaction. Benchmarking is learning through participation.
- It is not just networking through conferences, coffee breaks, telephone conversations, or browsing the Internet. Networking is useful and often a prelude to benchmarking, but it is no substitute for learning through participation, involvement, direct observation, and site visits.
- It is not quick or easy. Identifying, learning, adapting, and implementing best practices is hard work and takes time.
- There is not one unique "best" practice. A frequently asked question is, "How do you know who or what is best?" Rarely is one single "best" found in business, government, healthcare, or education. Best is a relative word, and what is best in one setting is not necessarily best in another.

  "Best practices" are those practices (there may be four, five, or more) judged to be "exemplary," "better," "good," or "successfully demonstrated." Most benchmarkers first work out a set of criteria for what they would judge to be "best" or "excellent." To help them arrive at a selected set of practices, they then look to literature research, surveys, peer and customer evaluations, site visits, and as much quantitative and qualitative data as they can gather.

By engaging in thousands of benchmarking studies, organizations have reported that major benefits can be achieved:

- Improvement in quality, productivity, outcomes, satisfaction, and reduced costs.
- Acceleration of restructuring and change.
- Prevention of costly "reinvention" when someone else has found a better way.
- Discovery of breakthroughs and new paradigms that yield not just incremental, small changes, but quantum changes.
- Creation of a sense of urgency when the size of performance gaps becomes known.

- Help in overcoming inertia, skepticism, complacency, and resistance to change.
- Evidence for setting higher, but attainable, goals for improvement based on objective evidence that such outcomes have been achieved elsewhere.
- Forced examination of your organization's processes, which can lead to improvements, as well as prioritization of improvement activities.
- Creation of sharing networks for future benchmarking, continuous learning, and improvement.

APQC'S EXPERIENCE

The American Productivity & Quality Center (APQC), home of the International Benchmarking Clearinghouse, is an internationally recognized nonprofit source for performance improvement and decision support—information and knowledge, networking, research, training, and advisory services. Organizations of all sizes and industries—business, government, education, and healthcare—partner with APQC to discover global best practices and to facilitate their development as "learning" organizations.

APQC began its foray into benchmarking in education in 1995 when Dr. C. Jackson Grayson Jr., APQC's chairman and founder, began investigating whether benchmarking was being conducted in education and whether benchmarking could help educators and policy makers improve the quality of learning, decision making, and strategy building in this critical area. His research revealed that, with a few exceptions, not many individuals or institutions in higher education were systematically exchanging best practices. This finding resulted in APQC establishing services designed to help education organizations transfer best practices through benchmarking—best practices not only from education but also from business, government, and healthcare. Today, many education organizations are moving across the benchmarking continuum (see Figure 2.1) because of external pressures from accrediting bodies, governments, and increasing competition, and because of a renewed emphasis on operating efficiencies. One way to accomplish this is through using an explicit benchmarking methodology to examine what other organizations currently are accomplishing within a specific program or service (e.g., structuring developmental education, processing online applications, or using technology in teaching).

To help institutions improve their performance, APQC has completed several consortium benchmarking studies in higher education. Some of these benchmarking studies[2] include:

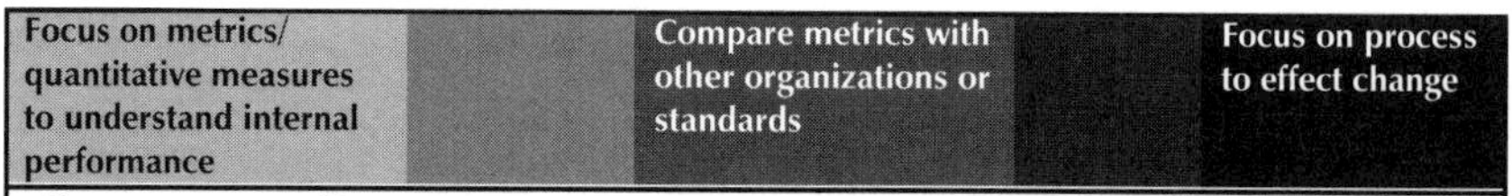

Focus on metrics/ quantitative measures to understand internal performance	Compare metrics with other organizations or standards	Focus on process to effect change

BENCHMARKING CONTINUUM

FIGURE 2.1

- **Faculty Instructional Development: Supporting the Use of Technology in Teaching** (the topic of this book), with the State Higher Education Executive Officers (SHEEO), and Dr. Tony Bates of the University of British Columbia.
- **Creating Electronic Student and Customer Services,** with SHEEO, and Dr. Mary Beth Susman of the Kentucky Virtual University.
- **Technology-Mediated Learning: Enhancing the Management Education Experience,** with AACSB—The International Association for Management Education, and Dr. Maryam Alavi of the Robert C. Goizueta Business School at Emory University.
- **Assessing Learning Outcomes,** with Dr. Morris Keeton, and University of Maryland University College.
- **Measuring Institutional Performance Outcomes,** with Dr. Peter T. Ewell of the National Center for Higher Education Management Systems (NCHEMS).
- **Institutional Budgeting,** with Dr. William F. Massey of the National Center for Postsecondary Improvement at Stanford University and the Pew Higher Education Roundtable Program.

One reason these initial benchmarking studies for higher education have been so popular is that benchmarking relates directly to the core values of education—learning, inquiry, data-based decision making, participation, open communication, learning by discovery, teaming, and collegial sharing.

CONSORTIUM BENCHMARKING METHODOLOGY

Because benchmarking is a systematic and disciplined process that requires specific steps to yield maximum knowledge and implementation, APQC has a methodology that provides the framework for each benchmarking study that APQC does, and its methodology is what differentiates it from other organizations. In an APQC consortium study, there are several key roles that individuals and organizations play:

1. APQC Study Team—This team of benchmarking specialists facilitates the entire consortium study, from the kickoff meeting through site visits and the concluding sharing session (or knowledge transfer session).

2. Study Sponsors – These self-selected organizations direct and fund the study, and their representatives play an integral part in each phase of the benchmarking process:

   - Provide input into survey development.

   - Complete screening survey.

   - Select best-practice partners.

   - Participate in site visits hosted by best-practice partners (facilitated by APQC).

   - Participate in the sharing session at the conclusion of the study, featuring best-practice partner presentations and roundtable discussions.

3. "Best-Practice" Partners – These organizations are identified through primary and/or secondary research as having innovative or "best" practices in specific areas. These organizations are invited to participate in the study as "partners." Their role differs from sponsors in that they may be selected to host site visits and present at the knowledge transfer session, but are not involved in the screening and selection phase of the study. In return for their time and knowledge, partner organizations participate in a study free of charge.

4. Subject Matter Expert—An individual with extensive expertise in the study topic who provides content knowledge for the duration of the benchmarking study.

APQC's consortium benchmarking studies have a twofold objective: to identify successful strategies, approaches, and tools for the process being studied; and to learn from innovative organizations that are using these strategies, approaches, and tools. The consortium process familiarizes participants with benchmarking through facilitated sessions, brings organizations together to create a rich, dynamic learning environment, and provides an ongoing network of partners with whom to continue benchmarking, sharing, and networking.

The methodology consists of four main phases that we will now briefly discuss.

Plan

During this phase of the study, the specific scope or context of the study is discussed, finalized, and clearly documented. It is important that the sponsors involved in the study participate in this step and that they agree on the final scope of what will (and what will not) be studied in the benchmarking initiative at hand. Additionally, the study surveys are developed and finalized, and the organizations to study (i.e., the potential best-practice partners) are identified. These organizations can be determined in numerous ways: use of secondary literature, nomination by study sponsors, or selection from a specific list, but they are all chosen based on criteria for best practice derived from the scope of the study. The scope drives everything related to the benchmarking effort; an organization should not be studied just because of its prestige or reputation.

Collect

Once the planning has concluded, the study moves into a general data collection phase. This phase takes numerous forms depending on the study and can include quantitative and qualitative data collection. For example, APQC has used phone interviews, interactive Web-based surveys, paper-based surveys, and face-to-face meetings (see page 35 for more information on site visits and their benefits to the study sponsors) to collect information from those innovative organizations chosen for in-depth study. Again, it is critical to ensure that the questions asked are designed to measure the processes delineated in the scope of the study, and that the data and information being collected will be useful once they are gathered, separating the "nice to know" versus "need to know" information.

Analyze

Once all the information has been collected, the task of analysis is at hand. What trends did benchmarking teams uncover during the site visits? What processes were truly innovative? And most important: which practices are adaptable given the sponsors' current organizational structures and cultures? The results of the analysis are often presented in face-to-face meetings with key stakeholders and project sponsors as well as through written reports.

Adapt

Analyzing and reporting the data are often easier than adapting the best practices learned. Achieving buy-in for change can be difficult, but change is more likely to be successful when a diverse team from within the sponsor organization is involved throughout the study, including attending site visits, because the shared experiences and the direct observations of workable innovation spur people to move beyond talk. APQC has found that when adapting and implementing best practices, sponsor organizations typically discover a whole new set of questions to address (e.g., "Yes, we've improved our course registration process, but now how do we improve course add-drop procedures?"). After successfully completing a first (and usually smaller-scale) benchmarking project, organizations often "graduate" to more complex benchmarking projects. As a result, the benchmarking process does not end with the adaptation phase. Instead, benchmarking tends to occur as a cycle, starting with planning, moving to collecting, analyzing, and adapting, and then starting all over with planning again.

FACULTY INSTRUCTIONAL DEVELOPMENT: SUPPORTING FACULTY USE OF TECHNOLOGY IN TEACHING BENCHMARKING STUDY

In 1996, APQC and SHEEO initially formed a partnership to find best practices in education through the use of benchmarking. The first study the two organizations conducted together was "Electronic Student Services: Learning from Business and Education," which concluded in May 1997. The second study from the APQC/SHEEO partnership—the basis of this book—entitled "Faculty Instructional Development: Supporting Faculty Use of Technology in Teaching," was completed in November 1998. Dr. Tony Bates from the University of British Columbia provided content expertise throughout the course of the study.

The purpose of this multiorganization benchmarking study was to identify and examine innovations, best practices, and key trends in the area of supporting the use of technology in teaching and to gain insights about the processes involved. This study aimed to enable sponsors to direct their own faculty instructional development processes more effectively and identify any performance gaps. It also afforded sponsors the opportunity to gain a better understanding of issues and challenges involved in implementing technology-enhanced education. Fifty-three institutions, businesses, and government agencies (this number includes study sponsors and best-practice partners) participated in the study by attending a series of planning sessions, completing data-gathering surveys, and attending or hosting on-site interviews. Seven of the organizations were identified (see the section on the review meeting for an explanation of the selection process) as having an exemplary process for supporting the use of technology in teaching and were invited to participate in the study as benchmarking "best- practice partners" at no charge to their organization.

THE BENCHMARKING PROCESS

The Faculty Instructional Development study followed APQC's internationally recognized consortium benchmarking methodology, described briefly earlier. This section will focus on the main events that occurred along the course of this study:

- Planning and Kickoff Meeting: securing sponsor participation, kick-off meeting, screening survey development
- Screening Process: initial survey of candidate best-practice organizations
- Review Meeting: blinded selection of best-practice partners
- Site Visits: in-depth qualitative information collected
- Analysis and Final Report: all the collected data is reviewed and key findings generated
- Sharing Session: concluding meeting of the study with all sponsors and best-practice partners

The flowchart in Figure 2.2 illustrates the order in which the main events of the study proceeded.

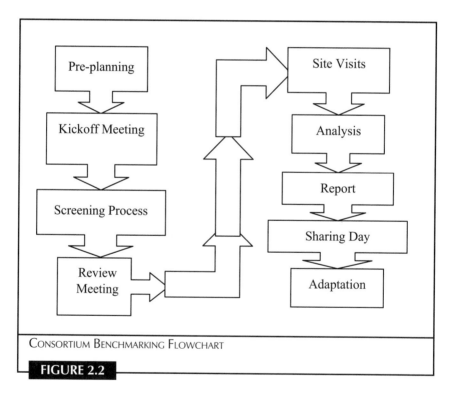

CONSORTIUM BENCHMARKING FLOWCHART

FIGURE 2.2

Planning and Kickoff Meeting

At the beginning of the study planning phase, APQC and SHEEO identified organizations, both higher education and business, that were interested in this topic and secured their participation in the study as fee-paying study "sponsors." The APQC study team also conducted some needs analysis to uncover the issues sponsoring organizations were struggling with in the faculty instructional development realm.

The study officially commenced with the April 16–17, 1998, kickoff meeting at APQC's facility in Houston, Texas. At this meeting, all the study sponsor organizations' representatives came together as a group to refine the study scope, create criteria to identify best practice, and brainstorm screening survey questions. The day-and-a-half meeting began with welcomes and introductions of all key study players.

Key study players included APQC representatives Marisa Brown, Kimberly Lopez, Peggy Odem, and Matt Sieger, who were primarily responsible for facilitating this benchmarking study. Both Dr. James R. (Jim) Mingle and Dr. Rhonda Martin Epper from SHEEO were integrally involved in the entire study and served as content advisors. Also, as mentioned earlier, Dr. Tony Bates of the University of British Columbia provided subject-matter expertise.

The sponsor organizations that engaged in this seven-month benchmarking process were:

Alabama Commission on Higher Education
Auburn University Montgomery
California State University System
    CSU Long Beach
    CSU Monterey Bay
    CSU Sacramento
    CSU San Bernadino
    CSU San Marcos
    San Francisco State University
    San Jose State University
    Sonoma State University
Connecticut Department of Higher Education
    Connecticut State University System
    University of Connecticut
Florida Gulf Coast University
Kentucky Council on Post Secondary Education
    Northern Kentucky University
    University of Louisville
    Western Kentucky University
    Kentucky Community and Technical College System (KCTCS)

Microsoft Corporation

Minnesota State Colleges and Universities
  Bemidji State University
  Fergus Falls Community College
  Normandale Community College
  Northland Consolidated Community and Technical College
  Rochester Consolidated Community and Technical College
  South Central Technical College
  Winona State University

New Mexico Commission on Higher Education
  San Juan College
  Eastern New Mexico University

Oklahoma State Regents for Higher Education
  Tulsa Community College
  Southeastern Oklahoma State University
  Oklahoma City Community College
  Murray State College
  University of Central Oklahoma
  University of Oklahoma
  Rose State College

Systems & Computer Technology Corporation (SCT)

University & Community College System of Nevada
  University of Nevada, Las Vegas

University of North Carolina

University of Wisconsin System
  University of Wisconsin—Milwaukee
  University of Wisconsin—Eau Claire
  University of Wisconsin—Colleges

Virginia State Council of Higher Education
  Virginia Tech

At the kickoff meeting, the subject-matter experts (Dr. Bates and SHEEO) engaged in dialogue with the consortium about various perspectives on faculty instructional development, and APQC presented an overview of the consortium methodology. Then the consortium participants refined the study focus areas (current institutional context, teaching and learning issues, organizational issues, policy and strategic issues, and performance evaluation) and collaboratively agreed on the following study scope. The study scope is the foundation on which the best-practice criteria and data collection tools are built.

Current Institutional Context
  Institutional vision for teaching via technology
  Campus technology infrastructure
  Current technology for teaching
  Technical support for faculty
  Faculty development arrangements

Teaching and Learning Issues
  Institutional philosophy for teaching and learning
  Technical skills
  Pedagogical skills
  Instructional design skills
  Project management skills
  Matching appropriate technology to learning objectives

Organizational Issues
  Overall organizational structure to support faculty development
  Reward systems
  Faculty workload
  Faculty development activities

Policy and Strategic Issues
  Funding levels
  State funding mechanisms
  Institutional funding mechanisms
  Cost/benefit analysis
  Scalability of products
  System level/consortium approaches (sharing revenue and cost)
  Outsourcing
  Mechanisms for faculty participation in policy and decision making
  Finding people with the right skills
  Collective bargaining, copyright, and intellectual property
  Program/curriculum review (institutional and state level)
  Strategic partnerships (e.g., K–12 collaboration)
  Technology standards/uniform policies for faculty development within and
    across campuses

Performance Measurement
  Input measures
  Output measures
  Alignment of performance measures with institutional goals

The sponsors also gave input as the group established criteria for best practice
(based on the study scope, these criteria are those characteristics that should be
evidenced by the best-practice partners). These criteria served as the standard

against which screening survey responses were evaluated. They helped the members of the consortium determine which schools, colleges, or companies should be selected for site visits.

The criteria for best practice, as decided by the sponsors, were:

- Centrality to mission.
- Program is organized around a philosophy/set of principles.
- Explicit vision for use of technology in teaching.
- Program has affected a significant number of faculty in department, college, or institution.
- Faculty instructional development is part of the culture.
- Project team approach (versus "Lone Ranger").
- Product oriented.
- Scalability of products.
- Productive use of resources (outcomes for money spent).
- Impact on individual faculty member.
- High level of faculty ownership.
- Demonstrated faculty satisfaction (customer focus).
- Reward structure supports faculty development initiatives.
- Differential strategies for different stages of faculty "readiness."
- Technology needs/utilization assessment has been conducted.
- Program encourages collaboration between faculty.
- Institution has a good balance of both discipline-based and skills-based programs.
- Focus on pedagogy and the learning process.
- Demonstrated positive impact on student learning.
- High level of dissemination.
- Campus technological capability.

The sponsors also selected criteria specifically for any business, government, or healthcare organizations that might be screened for best-practice partner. Those criteria were:

- Business demonstrates commitment to employee training.
- A core philosophy of learning.
- Strategically positioned in the company.
- Demonstrated employee/customer satisfaction.
- Demonstrated positive impact on employee learning.
- Business is not technologically oriented, but its success depends on training employees to effectively use technology.
- Business has highly educated, autonomous, professional employees.
- The product or services are knowledge intensive.
- Collaborative approaches.

This enabled APQC, SHEEO, and Dr. Bates to develop a list of potential best-practice candidate organizations through primary and secondary research. Suggestions were compiled from this research, as well as from periodicals, industry journals, and knowledge from sponsors. The result was a list of 80 potential best-practice organizations.

At the kickoff meeting, the sponsors also generated questions for the study's screening survey. This survey was finalized in an iterative process among the study team members and the subject-matter experts. It was finalized after a pilot team of some of the sponsors had a chance to review it as well. The function of the pilot team is to review the survey and provide feedback on it (i.e., Does this question or term need further clarification? Is this question too vague or ambiguous? How long did the survey take to complete?) The questions on the screening survey were mostly close-ended and were designed to elicit essential information that would enable the members of the consortium to select the organizations that truly seemed to be best practice or best-in-class. The screening survey functioned as a litmus test to determine best-practice partner organizations through quantitative, objective questions.

Screening Process

Once the screening survey was finalized, APQC then contacted all eighty of the candidate best-practice organizations (from the list generated by APQC, SHEEO, Dr. Bates, and the study sponsors) and asked them to participate in the project. Participation involved completing the screening survey and, if selected as a best-practice partner by the sponsor consortium, then hosting a one-day on-site visit for representatives from the study team and sponsor organizations. Two very similar and parallel surveys were administered to both for-profit organizations and nonprofit educational institutions. Selected organizations were also showcased at the sharing session, the study's finale.

Of eighty organizations invited to complete the screening survey, 43 did so for an overall response rate of 54%. APQC team members put all survey responses into a matrix that showed each organization's answer to all survey questions. Organizational identities were removed from the matrix so that the consortium members could select best-practice sites from the data alone, on the basis of described practices rather than on reputation or image. To assist sponsors in analyzing the blinded data, APQC also created a brief profile for each responding organization based on the survey answers.

Review Meeting

In a process facilitated by APQC team members, the consortium reconvened in late July 1998 for the review meeting. The major activities at this meeting for the sponsors included reviewing all the results of the screening process and

selecting best-practice partners. Responses from the education surveys were
analyzed and presented to the study sponsors at the meeting. Because not all
the data had been collected from the business and government organizations at
the time of the meeting, the data was not presented to the sponsors at that time.
Once all the business and government data had been collected from the
participating potential partners, it was dropped into a matrix parallel to the one
created for the education surveys and sent on to the sponsors to review and
analyze. The sponsors used an online selection process to determine the
business and government partner organizations. Organizations that completed
the screening survey represented both two-year and four-year institutions of
higher education as well as business and government organizations. Members
of the consortium combined qualitative and quantitative data to get a complete
picture of the candidate best-practice organizations. The subject-matter experts presented their "critic's choices" to the sponsor participants based on an
assessment of the survey data collected, and sponsors had opportunities for
discussion and dialogue and ultimately made their own independent selections.
The summation of the votes from the consortium as a whole led to the final
selection of best-practice partners.

Once the partners were selected, sponsors began preparing for site visits at
the selected partner organizations by reviewing APQC's roles and protocols for
the various parties participating in the site visits (sponsors, partners, APQC,
and SMEs) and generating open-ended, qualitative questions for the site visit
discussion guide. The questions on the site visit discussion guide were organized according to the major focus areas, or scope, of the study, and the
document took its final form again following an iterative process of input and
feedback from the subject-matter experts, sponsor pilot team (individual sponsors who volunteered to review the discussion guide and provided feedback for
further improvements or revisions to the study team), and APQC.

One important note is that the term "best practice" should not be miscon-
strued as a blanket seal of approval that an organization is outstanding in all
aspects. First, best practice for this study was defined by the consortium at the
kickoff meeting through the discussion of criteria for screening best-practice
partners. Second, the only process studied was faculty instructional development, not the overall organization. Therefore, the organizations were identified as having innovations in the focus areas of this study, not necessarily across
the board. This study looked at best processes for faculty instructional development; it did not try to identify best institutions.

Sponsors selected seven best-practice partner organizations:
Five educational institutions
One business
One government agency

The best-practice partners chosen were:

1. Arthur Andersen Performance and Learning (St. Charles, IL)
2. Bellevue Community College (Bellevue, WA)
3. California State University—Center for Distributed Learning (Sonoma, CA)
4. Collège Boréal (Sudbury, Ontario, Canada)
5. U. S. Air Force Air Command and Staff College (Montgomery, AL)
6. University of Central Florida (Orlando, FL)
7. Virginia Tech (Blacksburg, VA)

Partner organizations received significant benefits in return for their participation in this APQC and SHEEO benchmarking study. Some of the benefits included:

- "Best-practice" recognition by an unbiased, nonprofit third party.
- The ability to benchmark processes against other best-in-class performers.
- References to their organization's excellence in published reports, press releases, and/or articles.
- Interaction with subject matter experts.
- Networking and learning from other best-practice partners and study participants.
- Showcasing innovative practices to peers and potential clients.
- Building credibility for processes when reporting to senior administration.
- Keeping abreast of the latest information and practices.

Site Visits

All seven of the organizations selected as best-practice partners in this study hosted site visits at their locations between September and October 1998. Sponsors had the opportunity to sign up and attend the site visits to gain firsthand, tacit knowledge from the best-practice partners. The list of questions to be asked at the site visits was sent to the best-practice partners ahead of time to allow them to prepare and invite the appropriate people from within their organizations to participate in the event. Each interview was facilitated by a member of the study team and was structured to follow the organization of the site visit discussion guide. Benchmarking study site visits are designed to collect detailed, qualitative information in a question-and-answer format. A typical APQC site visit to a higher education institution lasts approximately six to seven hours; most corporate site visits are about four hours in length.

While a great deal of the information learned during the site visit process was contained in the final report, there were some additional benefits to sponsors from visiting the sites firsthand. Some of these benefits included:

- Tacit knowledge derived from face-to-face experience.
- Meeting the key players in the faculty instructional development process.
- Ability to ask specific questions as time allows.
- Networking with other sponsors/partners.

Post-site visit activities included having each sponsor representative who attended a site visit complete a debriefing form to record their impressions and reactions to the visit. The APQC team then created a formal site visit report that captured the essence of all the best-practice partners' answers to each question on the site visit discussion guide. The set of all seven site visit reports was distributed to all sponsors and best-practice partners in the study.

Analysis and Final Report

After the site visits were completed, the study team gathered all the information gleaned through the course of the study—including screening survey data, site visit reports, and sponsor site visit debriefing forms—and analyzed it for key findings, innovative practices, and enablers. The goal was to find out what factors have contributed to the partners achieving their best-in-class performance. The report identified 14 key findings, with each finding followed by explanation and examples from specific best-practice partner organizations. The final report also included an executive summary with an overview of the topic and study background, as well as highlights of the methodology. Following the sections dealing with the findings, there was a section with brief profiles of each best-practice partner, highlighting the organization's history and background, main uses of technology, faculty instructional development activities, and key lessons learned.

The final report also contained a special section written by some of the study sponsors. During the faculty instructional development benchmarking study review meeting in July 1998, the sponsors were faced with the challenge of selecting seven best-practice organizations from more than 40 candidates. After the consortium members selected the best-practice organizations for this study, they decided there were still many intriguing aspects to organizations that were not selected as best-practice partners. It was proposed by the consortium that mini-case studies be conducted to further analyze some of the unique aspects of several organizations in the initial screening pool.

The mini-case studies that were contained in that section of the final report represented a significant effort by several of the sponsors of the faculty instructional development consortium benchmarking study. The contributors were interested in learning more about the organizations they studied and volunteered to conduct this research on their own.

Sharing Session

At the conclusion of the study on November 19–20, 1998, a one-and-a-half day interactive conference was held in Houston to showcase the best-practice organizations and release the results of the study contained in the final report. This sharing session (also known as a knowledge transfer session) was an excellent opportunity for sponsors and best-practice partners to learn from each other and network with other organizations. Attendees at the sharing session included representatives from both the sponsor and best-practice partner organizations. Activities included best-practice presentations, breakout groups, and some initial action planning for sponsors.

The goals of the sharing session included the following:

- Provide a forum for exchange of best practices and presentation of study results.
- Facilitate networking among the entire consortium group, including sponsors and partners, in a collaborative learning environment.
- Hear presentations from best-practice partners and subject-matter experts.
- Ask follow-up questions of visited partners and other study participants.
- Exchange business cards and receive attendee list to promote networking after the study concludes.
- Provide feedback on the overall study process.
- Generate and submit ideas for future study topics and areas of interest.

Adapt and Implement

The sharing session was the first time that sponsors came together with other representatives from their own organizations (some of whom had participated in the study and some of whom were coming into the study for the first time) to lay the groundwork for steps to be taken after they returned home to implement some of the findings from the study. Adaptation and improvement resulting from the best practices identified throughout the consortium study occurred after the sponsor organization representatives took the learnings back to their organizations and began to work on improving their faculty instructional development processes.

CONCLUSION

Benchmarking has existed for many years, but recently it has gained increased publicity in the education arena due to many factors, including accreditation mandates, increased attention to operating efficiencies, and other problems and opportunities of a magnitude academia has never faced before. As demands grow for higher education to show process improvements, innovative colleges and universities may continue to turn to benchmarking to find solutions to their problems. Benchmarking delivers its best results when organizations are ready to entertain new and novel models for their practices and procedures. The APQC and SHEEO consortium benchmarking study on Faculty Instructional Development: Supporting Faculty Use of Technology in Teaching, where colleges and universities looked at their peers and others outside of higher education, is a true example of innovative "outside-the-box" process improvement.

NOTES

1. "Corporations Find Safety-Quality Link," *National Underwriter* 101, no. 30 (July 28, 1997).

2. Reports from these studies are available for purchase from APQC at www.store.apqc.org or by calling 800-776-9676.

CHAPTER 3

Institutionalizing Support for Faculty Use of Technology at the University of Central Florida

Joel L. Hartman and Barbara Truman-Davis

W hen we think about faculty using technology in their teaching, our attention often turns to the mechanical elements of introducing and supporting technology in the classroom. This is certainly an important element without which faculty initiatives could easily be thwarted, but classroom use of technology alone does not lead to transformation.

There are faculty at every institution who will find a way to use technology in their teaching—and in other areas as well. On some campuses, this can be a struggle of Herculean proportions, while on others, all the elements necessary to support and encourage faculty teaching innovation with technology are present. Many institutions are, of course, between these extremes.

This case study discusses efforts under way at the University of Central Florida to bring faculty use of technology in teaching into the mainstream.

INSTITUTIONAL SETTING: THE UNIVERSITY OF CENTRAL FLORIDA

The University of Central Florida (UCF) characterizes itself as a metropolitan university because of its setting and the institution's focus on meeting the needs of the central Florida region. The university's main campus is located approximately 15 miles east of Orlando, with major branch campuses or attendance centers in Daytona Beach, Cocoa, Palm Bay, and downtown and south Orlando. A relatively young institution, UCF is growing rapidly: the institution's current student population of 32,000 is expected to reach 48,000 by the year 2010. Reflecting the metropolitan area, the average student age is 26, approximately 40% of the university's students are part time, slightly less than 10% reside on campus, and approximately 65% are transfers from Florida community colleges.

The university has 877 full-time and 293 part-time faculty. Consistent growth has led to a classroom shortage on campus requiring the rental of classrooms from a nearby public high school to support the increasing number of night classes.

UCF has had an association with technology since its inception. The university was created as Florida Technological University, with a mission to serve the high-tech demands of the emerging space industry. The institution is entrepreneurial, adjusting and adapting to change perhaps more rapidly than other more traditional universities. Faculty demonstrate a variety of teaching styles and preferences, but the use of technology has become pervasive in all departments. Nearly all faculty use e-mail to communicate with their peers, and many use e-mail to enhance communication with their students.

Use of the Web for instructional and administrative capacity has also been steadily increasing. The university's strategic planning efforts have resulted in recommendations for using technology in all aspects of the institution. Many of these recommendations are now being implemented within specific faculty development initiatives. (See http://pegasus.cc.ucf.edu/~ucfdist/strategic.html for more information about the plan.)

INSTITUTIONAL LEADERSHIP AND COORDINATION

Expedited planning and decision making has been a characteristic of UCF's distributed learning program. Elements that have made this possible include:

- Obtaining the commitment of the university's senior administrators, from the president through the college deans.
- Close collaboration between the two vice provosts responsible for distributed learning.
- Working with faculty in cross-disciplinary cohort groups.
- Providing central, coordinated course development and faculty development support.
- The distributed learning advisory committee.
- Support for ongoing assessment.
- Use of a nationally recognized consultant, who worked with our deans and planning groups to shape policies and directions.
- Coordination among key support units.
- A clearly articulated mission and vision.

UCF'S STRATEGIC PLAN: TEACHING WITH TECHNOLOGY

Information technology is integrated within the institution's strategic plan. There are more than 60 specific references to information technology (IT) and senior university administrators have identified IT as a means of achieving the institution's goals.

One of the university's five goals is to provide the best undergraduate education in Florida. The UCF *Strategic Plan 1996–2001* attempts to answer the questions of who UCF is, where it is going and how it will get there. Institutional responsiveness is part of the campus culture, as stated in the plan's vision statement:

> UCF is future directed and united in commitment: a dynamic university with opportunities to take risks; to investigate creative change; to develop collaborative, cooperative relationships; to form partnerships; and to implement technological innovation.

Faculty use of technology occurs as a four-stage process:

1. Access   Do faculty have access to the basic tools of technology (e.g., computers, software, networks, and network services)?
2. Awareness   Are faculty aware of the existence of these resources and do they understand the ways they can be applied to their work?
3. Mastery   Do faculty have the skills needed to use technology resources in ways that are relevant to their teaching and scholarly work?
4. Application   Elements 1 through 3 allow faculty to apply technology, as appropriate, in their daily lives. Only when faculty achieve some level of mastery, or proficiency, with a particular technology can the application of that technology follow.

An institution wishing to create an environment that fosters faculty use of technology in teaching and scholarship must address all four of these elements. UCF has put in place orientations and faculty development programs to assist faculty from the day they join the institution. Many of the programs are designed to meet the individual needs of faculty learning styles, while being scalable for institution-wide use. In addition to the face-to-face consultations and classes available for faculty to learn, many programs are being developed as just-in-time training or self-paced study available anytime, anywhere. These programs are described in later sections. As support units refine their program offerings, a comprehensive learning system emerges, creating a climate of continuous learning across campus. Enthusiasm for teaching with technology gradually infects faculty peers, replacing skepticism with curiosity. Learning communities develop across disciplines through e-mail, conferencing, brown bag lunches, and similar events. As faculty master and apply technology, its use becomes a natural and accepted part of the campus culture.

TECHNOLOGY INFRASTRUCTURE

UCF has made significant investments in technology infrastructure, faculty and student support services, and organizational development to support faculty use of technology in teaching. Networking has become a core strategy for the university as it strives to serve a growing student population over an increasing geographic area and expand into new areas of technology-supported teaching, research, and administrative services. Although UCF was recognized in 1998, 1999, and 2000 as among the nation's "100 Most Wired Campuses" by *Yahoo Internet Life* magazine, our goal is to be more than simply a "wired campus." UCF is using network technology to create a sense of community, extending "7 by 24" access to information, services, and people to all students and employees, wherever they may be. These resources serve as platforms or tools that individual faculty can use to enhance their teaching or scholarly work.

In 1996, the university completed a campus networking project, through which all faculty and staff offices not previously connected were provided with access to the campus backbone network. New premise wiring, optical fiber, and network components were implemented throughout the campus to establish universal network connectivity. At the same time, the network backbone was upgraded from Ethernet to ATM operating at OC-12 (622 Mbit/second), with distributed 100 Mbit/second Ethernet switches providing high-speed connections to the desktop. UCF is a charter member of Internet2, and has played an active role in the advancement of education and research networking in Florida.

Emphasis has been placed on development of an ever-expanding suite of core network services. Today, these consist of electronic mail, World Wide Web, the full range of Internet utilities (e.g., telnet, FTP, etc.), extensive online library information resources, image processing, and online course delivery. Access to UCF information and services is made available through the university's main Web site (http://www.ucf.edu) and services such as PO-LARIS (https://polaris.ucf.edu), a Web interface to administrative services for students, faculty, and staff. These resources are available to all UCF network users. All central servers are regularly upgraded, and new servers added to accommodate the growth in both users and online information.

Access to online courses is viewed as one of the standard network services. A central server cluster hosts all online courses and supports more than 1,000

WebCT accounts (most of which are online courses), with more than 28,000 registered users.

A system of universal access was implemented in 1995, whereby all UCF students are provided with network and e-mail accounts from the point they are admitted. These accounts are maintained past graduation. All faculty and staff are also assigned network and e-mail accounts from the point of hiring. The pool of supported user accounts now exceeds 50,000 users.

A major effort has been undertaken to expand and modernize campus public computer labs, and currently more than 1,200 recent-vintage public PCs are available for student use. Lab computers are upgraded on a three-year replacement cycle, and all labs are equipped with 100 Mbps network connections, dedicated software servers, and free high-speed laser printing. Trained consultants are available in all public labs. Labs are open and help desk support is available to UCF students and faculty 18 hours a day, including telephone, Web, and walk-in assistance.

Classrooms are being upgraded for multimedia presentation through two parallel programs. The first takes advantage of the rapid pace of campus expansion. Major academic buildings are being constructed at the rate of approximately one per year (UCF must add approximately 6,000 square feet of new classroom space each year to keep up with the growth in student population). These facilities are designed to provide the latest in communications and multimedia presentation technology, and all instructional and meeting spaces are fully equipped. A companion program—the Classroom Improvement Project—provides annual appropriations for multimedia upgrades to existing classrooms. As a result of these dual efforts, more than 50% of all UCF classrooms are now capable of full multimedia presentation, and the number is growing steadily. The multimedia classrooms are very popular with both faculty and students, and there is substantial demand for expanding their availability. All multimedia classrooms are designed with touch pad controls that are virtually identical campus-wide, making the rooms easy and consistent to use.

ORGANIZATIONAL INFRASTRUCTURE

Over the past five years, UCF has put in place an organizational model that has become very effective in promoting faculty use of technology. The university is fortunate to have many units whose mission is to support faculty efforts to use technology in teaching and learning. In addition to carrying out their specific programs, these units collaborate broadly across campus to enrich opportunities for faculty development, as shown in Figure 3.1.

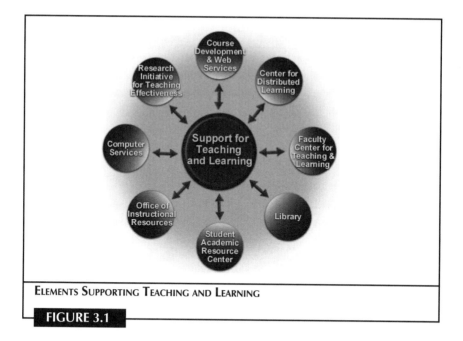

ELEMENTS SUPPORTING TEACHING AND LEARNING

FIGURE 3.1

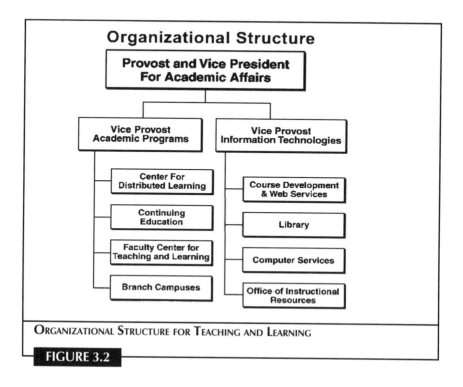

ORGANIZATIONAL STRUCTURE FOR TEACHING AND LEARNING

FIGURE 3.2

Structurally, all campus units involved with faculty development and training in the use of technology report to one of two divisions within the Office of Academic Affairs, as shown in Figure 3.2. Units reporting to the Vice Provost for Academic Programs include the UCF Center for Distributed Learning, Research Initiative for Teaching Effectiveness (RITE), Continuing Education, the Faculty Center for Teaching and Learning, and all off-campus delivery sites.

Reporting to the Vice Provost for Information Technologies and Resources (IT&R) are Course Development & Web Services, the Library, Computer Services and Telecommunications, and the Office of Instructional Resources. This organizational structure facilitates a comprehensive and coordinated response to the university's information technology needs. The Office of Information Technologies and Resources was formed in 1995. Although IT&R supports a wide range of administrative services, placement of this unit under the office of the Provost assures a high degree of emphasis and accountability for the support of teaching and learning.

Campus computing and telecommunications infrastructure and services are supported by Computer Services and Telecommunications (CS&T). This unit also operates the campus Computer Store; the Learning Center, a training facility for campus-standard software; and the CyberKnights program, a help desk and walk-in support center.

The Library has been given a prominent role in making available a wide array of electronic information services. More than 4,000 databases and full text resources are available online to UCF students and faculty (http://library.ucf.edu).

The Office of Instructional Resources (OIR) has been the primary source of multimedia support for classroom-based teaching as well as the unit responsible for the University's Interactive Television (ITV) network.

Recognizing the importance of Web-based learning and campus services, a new unit—Course Development & Web Services (CD&WS)—was created in 1997. Today, CD&WS is the primary instructional technology unit on campus, with responsibility for Web-based course and faculty development, and institutional Web services.

DISTRIBUTED LEARNING

The distributed learning initiative encompasses several modes of delivery. The following describes each mode:

"F"—Videotaped graduate engineering courses delivered to sites across the state as part of the Florida Engineering Education Delivery System (FEEDS).

"T"—Interactive television courses originated on campus and delivered through two-way interactive compressed video to UCF's branch campuses, and other attendance centers including the University of South Florida, and Florida Gulf Coast University.

"W"— Fully online Web courses delivered anytime, anywhere.

"M"—Media-enhanced Web courses that meet once a week on campus, with the remaining class activity conducted online. During fall 1997, data revealed that 75% of students taking fully online W courses were also taking face-to-face classes on campus. In response, UCF created a new type of Web course with reduced seat time. M courses have saved precious classroom space, increased interaction among students and faculty, and improved learning outcomes. The potential impact of M courses is campus-wide and has led to the conceptual evolution from distance to distributed learning.

"E"—Enhanced courses that require substantive use of the Web in addition to face-to-face classes. E-type courses do not reduce the number of class meetings.

Because many UCF students are working adults who live off campus, online courses that can be taken at flexible times makes higher education attainable for more of these individuals. Both students and faculty acquire advanced information management skills that remain with them throughout their careers.

Figure 3.3 represents growth in the number of students in online courses since their inception in fall 1996.

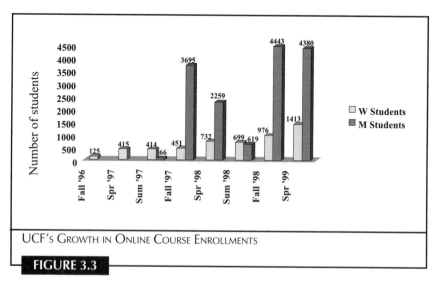

UCF's Growth in Online Course Enrollments

FIGURE 3.3

In addition to the M and W courses shown in Figure 3.3, approximately 120 E courses were offered during the fall 1999 term, more than the W and M courses combined. E courses are mostly a by-product of development of W and M courses. Faculty receiving grants to develop W and M courses frequently wish to use the Web in all their classes.

The rapid adoption rate of online learning has led to the creation of the UCF Virtual Campus. Online degree program enrollments are comparable to enrollments at branch campuses and growing more rapidly. As an economic model, this fact helps calibrate the resources necessary to support an online campus site. The Center for Distributed Learning has responsibility for planning and administering the university's Web-based, interactive television, and video-based academic programs. The Center also supports admissions and registration of students in off-campus and distributed learning credit programs, marketing support for off-campus and distributed learning courses, and coordination of university-wide accreditation planning for distributed learning programs.

UCF'S STRATEGY FOR LEARNING COMMUNITIES

One of the four statements of direction in the UCF strategic plan is to foster learning communities. An instructional model was adopted as the baseline for all online courses developed at UCF that originated from the first fully online course offered in summer of 1996. This instructional model included attention to student metacognition, learner support, and relied heavily on instructional design. The model emphasized computer-mediated communication (CMC) such as e-mail and conferencing rather than a content-centric approach.

A faculty development initiative was created in the summer of 1996 to facilitate a learning community among faculty committed to develop online courses. Each semester, faculty cohorts exchanged messages via online conferences created by instructional designers. Faculty shared their concerns, fears, and experiences that added to the baseline instructional model preventing common mistakes and facilitating adoption of best practices. This program evolved into the IDL6543 faculty development course now offered twice a year. A cultural change has developed leading to transformed course delivery that meets the needs of a metropolitan student population, eager to participate in online learning. Our data reveal that faculty satisfaction is correlated with the amount and quality of student interaction in online courses. Well-trained faculty learn to facilitate new forms of interaction not often possible within face-to-face classes. Spontaneous learning communities emerge across disciplines as students begin conferencing before class begins and do not stop after class has finished. The development of just-in-time, online learning opportunities helps fulfill the strategic plan's goal of using information technology to promote student-centered learning and personalize delivery of administrative services.

WALKING THE TALK: TRANSFORMATIVE FACULTY DEVELOPMENT

Many faculty development programs use workshops, guest speakers, or walk-in consultation. These offerings are relevant and useful, but often do not lead to the cultural change required to achieve a transformative integration of technology into teaching and learning. Individual consultation is difficult to scale up for enterprise-wide delivery of services and is frequently referred to as the "boutique approach." Course Development & Web Services staff began a program to teach faculty about systematic development of online courses with an emphasis on instructional design. "Walking the Talk" using technology to model online course delivery and management became the university's model for systematic faculty development.

IDL6543: Interactive Distributed Learning for Technology Mediated Course Delivery is an eight-week faculty development program designed to prepare faculty to develop and deliver interactive learning environments online. The program supports mainstream faculty as well as early adopters and innovators. Instructional designers create the IDL6543 curriculum and enhance it regularly through faculty feedback. The course combines face-to-face class meetings, hands-on labs, online modules, consultations with instructional designers, and homework activities. The IDL6543 class helps faculty develop one module of the course they plan to deliver online.

The IDL simulation course format evolved to its present state after it became apparent that faculty needed much more time to reconceptualize the learning possibilities presented in teaching online. Many faculty also needed referrals to additional training to bring their technology skills up to the level required to successfully participate in the class. The course format fosters collaboration and experiential learning among participants, leading to greater transformation of all teaching and learning. As soon as possible after faculty are identified for IDL participation, an instructional designer is assigned to be a consultant and act as liaison between the faculty and the production support staff. Faculty feel more assured by having a single point of contact to ask questions.

An initial needs assessment is conducted to gauge the level of the faculty member's technical skills, the adequacy of their computing equipment, and the needs of the course they will be developing. Faculty are provided with funds to purchase a new computer (if needed), and software is usually installed just prior to the class. A camera and audio setup is also provided to support desktop videoconferencing using NetMeeting and faculty are encouraged to use these tools to collaborate with their instructional designer. Several lengthy trips from branch campuses have been avoided by using desktop videoconferencing.

Faculty who receive support to develop online courses are expected to participate in the IDL6543 faculty development program and work with staff from the Course Development unit to design and develop their online course materials. As faculty go through IDL6543, they build activities and Web pages for use in their courses. Participants receive expert assistance with course design and production assistance by CD&WS's production staff. CD&WS was created to support the IDL6543 faculty development program and has interdisciplinary teams of instructional designers and digital media designers, programmers called "Techrangers," and software engineers to assist with course production support. More than 200 UCF faculty have participated in the IDL6543 faculty development initiative, resulting in the creation of more than 400 online courses. Faculty attending IDL6543 report being rejuvenated in their teaching. Each semester faculty from various disciplines become involved, resulting in an instructional model that builds on itself through peer teaching. This development cycle creates an upward spiral that allows the instructional model to continuously improve over time.

Approximately 500 faculty have received support from CD&WS for their online teaching since summer 1996. In the fall of 1997, UCF adopted the use of WebCT, an online course management tool, and it has been widely adopted by all of the university's colleges. WebCT training is conducted throughout the year, and faculty may choose the level of mastery they feel most comfortable with. CD&WS received a grant in spring 1999, to extend its WebCT training throughout Florida. In fall 1999, UCF became one of 16 WebCT Institutes for regional WebCT training.

For each course that is developed through the UCF online learning initiative, one or more of the following outcomes must be achieved:

- Improve the quality of high-enrollment classes by enhancing interactivity through Web-based techniques.
- Enhance the retention (completion rates) in courses that traditionally have low student success by using Web-based techniques to increase student-student and student-instructor interaction, providing automated tutorials and monitoring student progress using Web-based techniques.
- Enhance the efficiency of classroom utilization by using a combination of Web-based and synchronous course delivery. For example, a course that normally meets three hours a week would meet only once a week, with the remainder of course content delivered over the Web.

In summary, institutionalizing faculty development for online learning has provided these benefits:

- Provides experiential learning for faculty participants.
- Fosters cross-discipline sharing of teaching techniques.
- Builds learning communities among faculty and students.
- Creates lifelong learners among faculty.
- Stimulates discussion of the teaching and learning process.
- Allows peer evaluation of successes and failures.
- Exposes faculty to instructional tools and best practices.
- Models a combination of delivery techniques.
- Uses cooperative and collaborative learning techniques.
- Provides greater flexibility for busy faculty.
- Transforms teaching for more active learning delivery.

Faculty Development Units That Support Teaching with Technology

Faculty at UCF have many choices of where to go to learn to use technology and learn about teaching with technology. In addition to college support for using technology, there are five units that are involved in various aspects of faculty development. These units collaborate to deliver a wide range of services and programs.

The Computer Services Learning Center offers year-round classes on using software such as word processing, databases, presentation software, and e-mail. The Learning Center also administers a commercial computer-based training library that can be accessed online for self-paced study by all UCF faculty, students, and staff.

The Library holds year-round classes on using electronic resources for faculty and their students to promote information literacy. Many classes are scheduled in the beginning of the semester where librarians demonstrate database access for classes. The Library also holds classes on searching the Internet and using the Web to locate learning resources.

The Office of Instructional Resources (OIR) holds training sessions on classroom multimedia equipment. OIR provides production support such as creating PowerPoint presentations and loans out multimedia equipment upon request. OIR staff provide faculty training on the use of the equipment in Interactive Television (ITV) classrooms.

The Faculty Center for Teaching and Learning (FCTL) provides comprehensive orientation support to new faculty, adjuncts, and teaching assistants. The Center has a walk-in facility where any faculty member can receive support for their teaching in any modality.

Course Development & Web Services (CD&WS) provides support for faculty wishing to utilize the Web in their courses. The CD&WS staff conduct year-round training for using multimedia and Web-based authoring tools and deliver the eight-week IDL6543 class twice a year. CD&WS conducts year-round training on using the campus Web course management tool, WebCT, and also provides multimedia production support and support for online students. CD&WS instructional designers facilitate cultural change across disciplines for faculty with varying levels of technical skills and experience. As development activity increases through greater faculty participation, students are recruited each semester to become "Techranger" programmers. These students are actively involved in supporting course development and production, enabling faculty to focus more of their time on teaching and research.

INCENTIVES FOR FACULTY PARTICIPATION

Support for faculty use of technology has become highly institutionalized at UCF due to extensive planning and involvement in professional associations such as EDUCAUSE and the National Learning Infrastructure Initiative (NLII). Accordingly, the significant level of commitment to the goal of institutionalization is perhaps the primary reason for the rapid growth of distributed learning and faculty use of multimedia in the classroom, as well as the high degree of overall faculty satisfaction regarding these programs. Academic priorities and policy are set through collaboration between central administration, the college deans, and department chairpersons. This is accomplished through a combination of formalized planning and ensuring that technology remains a recurring agenda item for Council of Deans and Provost's staff meetings. This assures that continuous attention is focused on the subject.

The Office of Academic Affairs provides financial support for faculty participation in IDL6543, the faculty development program to prepare faculty to develop and deliver online courses. This process is managed by the Center for Distributed Learning, which issues course development requests for proposals (RFPs) twice each year. Approximately 60 faculty are selected to participate— 30 in the fall, and 30 in the spring. Each selected faculty member is expected to develop a minimum of one new online course

The Faculty Center for Teaching and Learning (FCTL), in collaboration with the other support units, sponsors a summer Faculty Institute and a winter Faculty Workshop that include extensive hands-on experience with developing instructional applications of technology. Faculty are provided stipends to support their participation in these events.

Faculty incentives are also provided through the Research Initiative for Teaching Effectiveness (RITE), the unit responsible for ongoing evaluation of the distributed learning initiative at UCF. RITE encourages faculty to participate in innovative instructional settings by providing them with assessment design assistance, instrument preparation, and data collection and analysis services. Research results are provided to the faculty in publication-quality format, and become the faculty member's intellectual property. Approximately half of all faculty engaged in online course activity have published or given conference presentations related to their work. Thus, the assessment effort has become a mechanism to successfully connect instructional innovation with the faculty reward system.

IMPACT EVALUATION

Since the inception of the distributed learning initiative in 1966, UCF has carried out a continuous assessment project to assess the impact of online classes. The assessment effort takes a coordinated approach to collecting data about student and faculty demographics, growth in enrollments and sections, student and faculty perceptions of teaching and learning online, and problems encountered while teaching and learning in the online environment. The results have been used to identify opportunities for improvements in faculty development, learner support, and technical support. Over the past year, learning styles of students in online courses have been studied with the goal of helping faculty address the needs of students with different learning styles. Plans are to enable students to determine their own learning styles and make informed choices about the types of courses they select.

Work is under way to assess student reactions to distributed learning according to learning style. Now in its third year, the assessment effort includes several dimensions focusing on students and faculty:

1. Student participation, success rates, and withdrawal rates in fully online and media-enhanced courses.
2. Impact of learning styles in the online environment.
3. Satisfaction of students and faculty with the online environment.
4. Demographic trends for students and faculty participating in online courses.
5. Developing strategies for faculty and student success in the online environment.
6. Faculty initiated research projects including:
   A. Teaching and assessing critical thinking online.
   B. Real time approaches to data collection.
   C. Quasi-experimental approaches to satisfaction and outcome assessment.
   D. The impact of online environments on the accreditation process.
   E. The impact of teaching high enrollment online classes.
   F. Changes in personal theorizing regarding approaches to teaching that result from online instruction.
   G. Effectiveness of various assessment techniques in the online environment.

For more information about UCF's Distributed Learning Impact Evaluation see http://reach.ucf.edu/~research.

FACULTY SATISFACTION

Although UCF's distributed learning initiative has been under way only four years, our experience and findings from our ongoing assessment efforts lead us to believe that the following factors contribute to faculty satisfaction, at least in our environment. These include:

- *Online Course Interaction.* Our studies repeatedly find that the quantity and quality of interaction in online courses, as reported by the faculty, have a strong, positive, statistically significant relationship to faculty satisfaction.
- *Reliable Infrastructure.* By maintaining a fast, reliable, well-maintained course server, faculty are relieved from the burden of finding a machine to host their courses, and from the duties of system administration.
- *High-Quality Faculty Development.* The IDL6543 faculty development program is continually being refined and extended. The program was recognized in 1999 as a best practice in a SHEEO-APQC North American benchmarking study of faculty development support for the use of technology. The IDL program helps faculty transform to a student-centered mode of learning suitable to the online environment.
- *Extensive Faculty Support.* In addition to IDL6543, faculty can rely on the Course Development unit to help create and maintain their courses. Although greater faculty independence is encouraged, this need not come before the faculty member is ready and willing to assume course maintenance responsibility. Also, faculty have a central unit to call on in the event of a technical anomaly.
- *Faculty Recognition and Incentives.* Faculty are recognized for their online work. For example, at the completion of each semester's IDL6543 program, an event is held in which each faculty member presents the course materials he or she has developed and discusses the course strategy and goals. Deans and senior administrators attend these presentations and thereby become familiar with the online work of the faculty.
- *Interdisciplinary Approach.* The IDL6543 program involves faculty from all colleges and a wide variety of disciplines. Faculty report that this is one of the few times they have had the opportunity to discuss teaching and learning with not only their own colleagues but also

those from other disciplines. The spirited discussions that occur are rated as one of the most beneficial features of the program.

- *Web Vets.* Faculty who have successfully taught online courses are heavily involved as guest presenters and mentors in the IDL6543 program. The ability of faculty just beginning to explore online learning to "hear it straight" from others more experienced plays a significant role in giving online courses credibility, as well as fostering best practices. Many of the faculty involved in online courses are senior faculty who report enjoyment from learning new ways to enhance student learning.

- *Student Support.* Student success is closely linked with faculty satisfaction. By providing enhanced support for students taking online courses, faculty are relieved of much of that burden and can focus on course content and flow. Student academic outcomes in the online environment can equal or exceed those of purely face-to-face classes, and improved student academic success associates positively with faculty satisfaction.

- *Assessment.* UCF has an extensive assessment effort under way to examine the processes, effectiveness, and outcomes of our online course initiative. The results of this effort yield significant insights into how the online process works and for whom. Armed with this information, faculty can be more confident about how to deal with individual students, and are aware that not all individuals succeed equally in the online environment. The results of the assessment effort are available to all, and the positive results being reported further add to the credibility of online courses as an effective learning environment.

- *Institutionalization.* We approach online learning not as a collection of unrelated, individual courses, but rather as a comprehensive, coordinated institutional initiative. Significant effort has been expended on putting all the necessary elements in place, including infrastructure, coordination, program development, faculty development support, and assessment. Further, the university's online effort is linked with specific institutional goals, which can be traced directly to the university's strategic plan. The university thus knows not only how it is engaging in online education, but also why.

- *Continuous Improvement.* All aspects of the online effort are continually being reassessed and improved. This, of course, must be balanced with the need for stability. By providing ongoing training for both faculty and staff, new tools and techniques can be quickly adopted.

Our ultimate goal for online learning is for it to become so commonplace that it is taken for granted. By emphasizing a quality, systematic, institutionalized approach, we believe that our online initiative is slowly (or perhaps not so slowly) creating an institution-wide transformation of teaching and learning. Further, we believe the day is not far away when courses that do not use such technology will become the exception.

This could not occur without a high degree of faculty participation and satisfaction, and we will continue to emphasize that outcome as one of the most important in our online endeavors.

COMPREHENSIVE LEARNER SUPPORT

The IDL6543 faculty development program has a complementary learner support component that comprises a Web site, ongoing technical support, and a CD-ROM. An internal strategic planning grant was awarded in the summer of 1997 to fund CD&WS and the Center for Distributed Learning to collaboratively develop the Pegasus Disc (Pegasus is UCF's logo). This CD-ROM provides software tools, tutorials, just-in-time UCF information, and a wizard to configure the user's PC to connect into the campus network. Today, all UCF students and faculty receive a copy of the Pegasus Disc during orientations. Another initiative to support teaching with technology was creation of the "CyberKnights." Full- and part-time staff work in campus computer labs to provide extended face-to-face, telephone, and online support for students and faculty needing assistance with their courses.

LESSONS LEARNED

Over the past three years, we have had many opportunities to reflect on our own mistakes and successes, and share our experiences with others. The following emerge as critical success factors, both in our own institution and others.

Organize for success. Faculty adoption of technology takes diverse forms, and once established can expand rapidly. Close cooperation and coordination among campus units with responsibility for supporting faculty development and technology services is essential. To achieve consistency, quality, and scalability, it is necessary to establish a central service coordination unit with sufficient resources to develop and apply standards and support the expanding volume of work that will result from increased faculty demand. Ultimately, the departments, colleges, and individual faculty will need to assume some level of responsibility for the creation and ongoing support of technology-based instructional resources. As this begins to occur, coordination between central IT and the academic units is of fundamental importance.

Build with scalability in mind. Faculty use of technology generally begins as a series of individual efforts by a few early adopters. Involving mainstream faculty requires an institutional response and both breadth and depth of support. Growing faculty adoption of technology creates a constant demand for increased facilities and support. Therefore, both the IT organizations and the infrastructure provided must be both highly scalable and reliable as usage increases. The techniques and tools used must also be scalable. Having to shift to more powerful software platforms and replace servers with larger machines can be disruptive.

Build consensus bottom-up and top-down. Ultimately, if faculty are to willingly adopt the use of technology, it must be on their terms. Faculty must therefore be in a position to provide input, recommendations, and ongoing feedback regarding the various technology resources available and their potential for enhancing teaching and learning. Faculty interest alone, however, does not always lead to success. Senior administrators must support increased use of technology and have an understanding of how technology relates to the institution's goals and objectives. They must also be prepared to make the sustained investments necessary to provide, maintain, and renew the infrastructure and faculty development resources needed to achieve quality outcomes.

Manage change. With technology, the one constant is change. Each new multimedia classroom has the latest hardware and software; each new online course is improved over the ones before it. New problems must be solved and new approaches created, requiring ongoing research and development. To give change direction, the institution must have a vision of where it wishes to go and at what pace. The downside of change manifests itself in discomfort for the users of technology and the increasing inventory of equipment and software that must be continually maintained and upgraded. It is the responsibility of the IT organizations to both lead change and help protect the faculty and other campus users from its negative aspects.

Continuous assessment is important. The instructional effectiveness of technology is sometimes taken for granted; that does not mean, however, that it should be. As faculty make increasing use of technology in teaching and as their roles begin to change, both faculty and administrators gain comfort from feedback that tells them what is being accomplished. To the extent that technology is being introduced to accomplish institutional objectives, assessment is necessary to measure effectiveness. As with any instructional improvement effort, the introduction of technology continually raises new questions and issues. Formative assessment allows practitioners the opportunity to make continuous improvements in tools and techniques.

FUTURE DIRECTIONS

The two cornerstones of UCF's faculty technology initiatives are classroom multimedia and online learning. Our long-term goal is to equip all classrooms, auditoria, and other learning spaces with advanced multimedia presentation facilities. Our design concept, however, is much broader than just equipment. We are attempting to make our classrooms "information transparent," that is, to facilitate the movement of information between the classroom and the outside world. In traditional face-to-face classroom settings, when the bell rings and the door closes, the instructional information space is defined by those present in the room. Technology makes it possible to interact with people and information anywhere, be it elsewhere on campus, in the local community, or globally. UCF's multimedia classroom design includes high-speed data network access, and voice and video lines to support audioconferencing and videoconferencing.

The three models of Web-delivered or Web-enhanced courses (W, M, and E) differ primarily with regard to the emphasis placed on the online component, and the degree to which this component replaces classroom "seat time." The fully Web-based model (W) is primarily an accessibility model, and will be expanded through the addition of additional online degree programs. The primary emphasis for UCF will be on the combined live-Web model (M), which appears to optimize both the face-to-face and online components and can produce significantly improved student learning outcomes. Further, this model scales well for both high and low enrollment courses. We anticipate that within the next few years, more than 90% of all courses at UCF will make use of Web-based resources and online collaboration tools. UCF's online course model emphasizes the development of learning communities, which is well suited to our distributed metropolitan student population.

Alongside the rapidly expanding online course initiative, the university plans to significantly expand the availability of student and employee Web services. The university's main Web site (www.ucf.edu) was redesigned over the past year. A major follow-on effort has been launched to expand the body of online information and services available. The coming service portal environment will be personalized and role-based; that is, individuals will be recognized and they can select the appropriate role (student, employee, alum, etc.) that applies to the particular services or transactions being sought. We further intend to implement online services as complete business processes, rather than discrete transactions. For example, students registering for classes will be prompted to see a list of required textbooks and offered an opportunity to purchase them online. They might also be shown links to images of the buildings and classrooms where their courses will be offered, maps showing the location of the buildings or adjacent parking, or links to the professors' home pages and the course home pages. Similar "pull-through" service clusters will be developed for other types of services.

SUMMARY

UCF's online initiatives have been recognized as a best practice for faculty development in teaching with technology by a 1998 benchmarking study conducted by the American Productivity and Quality Center (APQC) and the State Higher Education Executive Officers (SHEEO). The United States Distance Learning Association also recognized UCF for excellence as a best program in March 2000. The following factors are driving UCF's transformation of teaching with technology:

- Link initiatives to the institution's strategic plan.
- Lead through administrative support.
- Provide instructional design support.
- Facilitate learning communities to enhance learning and satisfaction.
- Support learners with and through technology.
- Assess continuously as a core process.
- Participate in professional societies such as EDUCAUSE and NLII.

Sustaining momentum gained through transformation of teaching requires continuous institution-wide commitment.

REFERENCES

The UCF Strategic Plan is available online at: http://pegasus.cc.ucf.edu/~ucfdist/ strategic.html

ACKNOWLEDGMENTS

The authors would like to acknowledge Frank Juge, Vice Provost of Academic Programs, Steve Sorg, Associate Vice President of the Center for Distributed Learning, and Chuck Dziuban and Patsy Moskal of the Research Initiative for Teaching Effectiveness for their continued contributions to the success of UCF's use of teaching with technology.

CHAPTER 4

The Evolution of Faculty Instructional Development in the Use of Technology at Collège Boréal, Ontario

Chantal Pollock, David Fasciano, Louise Gervais-Guy,
Daniel Gingras, Raymond Guy, and Renée Hallée

INTRODUCTION

In order to fully understand faculty instructional development in the use of technology at Collège Boréal, it is imperative to be aware of other influencing factors. The restructuring of the curricula, a humanistic model of learning, and new waves of technology all have had a major impact. Also, the perspective of learners will be included in the discussion because of the interrelationship between learners and faculty. It is difficult to discuss one without the other.

Collège Boréal is a five-year-old, publicly funded college in northern Ontario, Canada. It serves a population of 165,000 francophones (French-speakers). This represents 20% of the total population, scattered across a very large area, roughly 360,000 square miles or 85% of the province of Ontario. Boréal has seven campuses, plus another 15 access centers in different communities. It opened in 1995 after many years of lobbying by the francophone community and currently has approximately 1,500 full-time learners enrolled. It is the first French-language college in northern Ontario. Historically, few Franco-Ontarians pursued their studies at the postsecondary level. Thus, one of the challenges facing Collège Boréal is to create a new culture within the Franco-Ontarian population regarding postsecondary education.

From the very beginning, the ultimate goal of Collège Boréal was to become a highly reputable college and much in demand by learners, within five years. A once-in-a-lifetime opportunity was offered when Collège Boréal was officially recognized and appropriate funding made available. A start-up team was put in place two years before the official opening of the college. Procedures were established to allow francophone faculty and support staff from five community colleges located in northern Ontario who offered some French and bilingual programs to transfer to Collège Boréal. Having the mandate to offer programs in seven communities spread out over a large geographic area and to be financially responsible was quite a challenge. Collège Boréal took on the challenge by being very creative and implementing a number of strategies to bring about an academic transformation, by encouraging faculty to move from traditional to nontraditional teaching . It was established from the beginning that faculty would become facilitators as opposed to information givers, and that learners would be active participants in their learning.

Collège Boréal is funded exactly the same as the other Ontario colleges. Various sources of funding are available to Ontario colleges who meet the particular criteria. Collège Boréal has access to the following funds:

1. *General Purpose Operating Grant* This grant is distributed largely on the basis of the volume of instructional activity. All 25 Ontario colleges have access to this grant.
2. *Northern Grant* This grant recognizes that northern colleges have additional expenses related to the geography. Six northern colleges, five anglophone and 1 francophone, have access to this grant.
3. *Incremental Funding* This fund is made available to all three francophone colleges because it is more expensive to operate in the French language as a minority, within a mainly anglophone environment.
4. *Ontario Language Education Program* This fund is distributed to all three francophone colleges. In Ontario, francophone colleges were developed at a much later date than the anglophone colleges and therefore have some catching up to do.

Hence, Collège Boréal manages to bear the cost of its innovations through funding similarly available to other Ontario colleges.

RESTRUCTURING CURRICULA

The leaders of the start-up team understood from the very beginning that it was necessary to reorganize the curricula in order to initiate academic transformation. It was also obvious that faculty needed to be actively involved in every aspect of the process in order to have a buy-in. The curricula was overhauled by three major initiatives that included integrating the new directions of the Ontario Ministry of Education and Training, organizing the curricula in common and specialty cores, and developing the concept of continuous intake.

One year before the official opening of the college, the start-up team mobilized six teams to begin integrating the new directions of the Ministry of Education and Training and organizing the curricula in common and specialty cores. The teams were organized to gather together faculty who were working in programs that had an affinity with one another. The six teams represented the following families of programs: Business; Office Administration; Human Sciences; Technology; Natural Sciences; and Health Sciences. Each team consisted of a leader and faculty members who were still working in their respective original colleges. The leader of each team met regularly with a facilitator from the Collège Boréal start-up team to get guidance, discuss arising difficulties, and share some solutions. The leaders also met with their teams on a regular basis. The work was done during weekends and evenings. Some teams had members spread across different regions and either had to use audioconferencing or travel in order to do the work. All team members were still working full time at their originating college and working extra hours for Collège Boréal. To compensate these persons, a contract was signed between the team members and Collège Boréal, and they received an honorarium distributed in installments. Collège Boréal also covered traveling expenses.

The New Directions of the Ministry of Education and Training

On two occasions, a facilitator from the start-up team organized a workshop with an expert on the new directions of the Ministry of Education and Training, and all the members of the six teams participated actively. The new directions included integrating generic skills, general education courses, and vocational skills within the curricula. Generic skills refers to skills that are transferable such as interpersonal skills. General education courses make learners more rounded. For example, the course "Spanish Culture" could be a general education course within the Social Services Worker program. Vocational skills refer to specialty skills that are integrated in specialty courses. For example, the course "Social Law" could be a specialty course within the Social Services Worker program. The Ministry required all courses be expressed in learning outcomes, as opposed to objectives. To this day, some programs are still refining this process. This overhaul of the curricula had to be done by all the community colleges in Ontario; in other words, this was a province-wide initiative.

Common and Specialty Cores

Team members were also expected to organize the curricula in common and specialty cores for Collège Boréal. At the time, our intention was to offer 45 postsecondary programs at the main campus and 29 postsecondary programs in the regional campuses. In order to offer the 29 postsecondary programs in the regional campuses, common cores were developed in the following areas: Business, Office Administration, Human Sciences, Technology, and Natural Sciences. It was not possible to develop a common core in Health Sciences because the duration of the programs varied from one to three years and it was thus difficult to work into a common year.

Programs that had an affinity with one another were grouped together into a common core program. For instance, Chemical Technology, Environmental Technology, Construction Engineering, Electrical Engineering and Electronics Engineering were grouped within the common core of Technology. All campuses offered the first-year common core programs, while, the main campus offered the specialized second- and third-year programs. At this stage, faculty members made a lot of concessions within their work groups. The curricula were completely dismantled and rebuilt. Each team identified the common themes of the programs they were working with and incorporated these in courses for a common first year.

Although the common core programs presented many challenges, they also resulted in some interesting benefits. The attrition rate is low, since learners study in their home community in the first year, surrounded by their support systems, such as family members and friends. There are also financial benefits for the learners, since they do not have to pay for an apartment because they are still living at home for the first year. Also, learners have the possibility to switch programs after the first year if they discover an interest in another program. Finally, learners are able to obtain two diplomas within three years. For example, a learner who has graduated from the Social Services Worker program, requiring one common year and one specialty year, can then enroll in another specialty year in the Gerontology program.

The teams successfully developed the common and specialty cores for 29 programs before the official opening of Collège Boréal in 1995. It was a marathon effort. It is interesting to observe that even before the introduction of technology within the college, the whole curricula was restructured. We were to find that technology really enhanced the organization of the curricula into common and specialty cores. This will be discussed in another section of this chapter.

Continuous Intake

Shortly after the college opened its doors, we started to explore the possibility of making the programs more flexible. A faculty team was given time within their workloads to develop a model for continuous intake. The model required another restructuring of the curricula. Each course would need to be broken into smaller units and in some cases it would have meant dismantling the entire program into small units, regardless of the existing courses. As much as possible, the prerequisites for each unit would have been eliminated. This would have allowed learners to enter the program two to four times a year and to take the units in various sequences. In this model, it would have been imperative for faculty to accompany the learner right from entry, which could be at odd times, and to assist the learner to select appropriate units. Only four programs attempted to apply the continuous intake concept and some of these programs ran into difficulties managing the small units. In most cases, there was only one full-time faculty member to oversee the whole process and it became overwhelming. At this point, continuous intake in its pure form is still rare at Collège Boréal.

LIFELONG LEARNING IN THE HUMANISTIC MODEL

Lifelong learning is a process by which learners engage in activities with experts, their peers, and a given subject matter. Learning is a social activity that requires various levels of interaction. Collège Boréal refers to its humanistic model to identify landmarks in the topography of learning. The integration of four levels of interaction in each learning experience ensures a holistic learning outcome.

The four cornerstones of the humanistic model are dependence, counterdependence, interdependence, and independence. Each level of interaction is a dynamic component within a total learning experience. The learning mode may vary in importance and may be accessed in a varied sequence to meet the desired learning outcomes.

The dependence relationship for learners and faculty occurs during the presentation of a course's learning outcomes. Without this, no pertinent learning could occur. The dependence stage requires faculty to set goals and direct learning. Faculty are also dependent at this stage on the availability of resources for the development of support strategies.

Independence enables personal advancement along a learning path. The independent learner selects the pace, the place, and the mode of learning to develop maturity and self-proficiency. Faculty can also move independently in their development. Individual ideas and expertise are essential in applying personal strategies to integrate technologies.

Counterdependence is a normal component of a relationship in which learners challenge

and shape individual learning paths. Faculty may also express counterdependence both by challenging new directions and also by challenging the status quo. This component of learning may be overlooked, but is essential in improving quality and developing vision.

Interdependence is the key element that ensures timely and efficient interactions between learners, faculty, and other service providers who guide and assist throughout the learning process. This is one of the most rewarding components of learning. Interdependence taps into the value of teamwork and constructivism.

The dynamics of learning include these four relationships. The development of human potential has to focus on people and their interactions with respect to selected outcomes. Collège Boréal's humanistic learning model focuses on the development of competencies that include skills, knowledge, and attitudes for success in the workplace. This model was developed with learners in mind, but is readily applicable to faculty who become learners in new initiatives.

THREE WAVES OF TECHNOLOGY

Collège Boréal has fully experienced two waves of technology, videoconferencing and mobile computing, and is now in the process of experiencing a third wave, namely online learning. Videoconferencing is used in real time mostly for courses and whenever possible for meetings. Mobile computing provides a tool to enhance education, facilitate communication, and access information inside and outside the classroom. Online courses will be used to extend the classroom beyond the space and time boundaries.

In a span of five years, most faculty at Collège Boréal have been bombarded with technology nonstop. In most cases, technology has enhanced the learning process, but in some cases, technology has hindered it. The following sections will discuss thoroughly each wave of technology.

THE FIRST WAVE: VIDEOCONFERENCING

Collège Boréal is part of a consortium called the *Réseau franco-ontarien de l'enseignement à distance* (RFOED—Franco-Ontarian distance education network). This consists of three colleges and four universities throughout Ontario. The mandate of the consortium is to provide collective buying power, to resolve technological problems, and to offer opportunities for professional development for faculty and technical support staff. At Collège Boréal, there are now 20 videoconferencing sites spread out throughout all the campuses. Most videoconferencing classes are equipped with a document camera and an electronic board. A technician is available in each campus to assist faculty and learners to maximize the use of the technology and to troubleshoot when problems occur, since a malfunctioning videoconferencing system can be disastrous.

Videoconferencing is mostly used to offer common core courses to the regional campuses. It is not always possible to offer only face-to-face courses in the regional campuses. Sometimes the community does not have the specialized faculty necessary to offer the course and sometimes learner numbers are small. Therefore, in our regional campuses, about 50% of the courses in the common cores are offered face-to-face and the other 50% are offered by videoconferencing. Over an eight-month period, Collège Boréal offers about 130 videoconference courses. Courses are offered back to back, Monday to Thursday from 8:00 A.M. to 10:00 P.M., and Friday, from 8:00 A.M. to 4:00 P.M., practically nonstop. This represents about 1,000 hours of videoconferencing per week. When not in use for academic purposes, the videoconferencing systems are used for meetings by various groups within and outside the college.

Each semester, there are about 30 to 40 faculty members teaching courses through videoconferencing. A faculty member could have up to 30 learners in seven different campuses. Before the beginning of each semester, all faculty members are invited by the technician to attend a workshop on how to use the technology. The workshop takes on a very practical approach and allows faculty to manipulate many aspects of the videoconferencing systems such as microphones, cameras, document camera, and electronic board. At the beginning of the semester, the technician will remain in the class to assist faculty and then gradually move to peeking in the classroom several times to ensure that everything is running very smoothly. There is an in-house telephone in the videoconferencing classroom allowing faculty to communicate at all times with the technician, who is similarly equipped.

Two to three weeks after the onset of the semester, the faculty member is then approached by an educational consultant to participate in a workshop in which instructional issues are discussed. The workshop is done at this time because most part-time faculty are hired just before the onset of the semester. At that time, they have an urgent need to deal with the technical aspects as opposed to the instructional aspects. Throughout the semester, the educational consultant will touch base with the faculty member to identify whether assistance is required.

Many courses from various disciplines are taught via videoconferencing such as Business, Office Administration, Human Sciences, Technology, Natural Sciences, and even Health Sciences. Some faculty members are very creative—for instance, having electronic labs within the videoconferencing classroom. Learners mount various circuits and demonstrate to faculty by using the document camera. Some faculty members are experiencing some difficulty with courses that depend mostly on the affective and body aspects of communication, for example, the course "Human Relations."

Faculty members teach at the most one to two courses using this technology each semester. There is an attempt to maintain the same faculty member with the same course for a period of two to three years. This allows the faculty to perfect the course from year to year. Faculty members who are good facilitators and promote interaction through various learning activities are usually very successful when using videoconferencing. On the other hand, faculty members who are very traditional in their teaching tend to experience a variety of problems with the learners, such as lack of participation, frequent absenteeism, and discipline problems. When a faculty member experiences problems in a face-to-face context, these same problems are amplified in the videoconferencing context. Faculty members have access to funds to travel from one campus to the other in order to meet learners face-to-face at least once during the semester. It is always wise for faculty to prepare a plan B in case of technological problems, although they now rarely occur.

Learners also benefit from a workshop with a technician, where there is an opportunity to manipulate the various pieces of equipment. Also, they receive a workbook that they go through as a group and can keep handy for quick reference. This workbook includes various technological tips for video–conferencing use and learning strategies for distance learners. Learners also have access to a learning center in each campus where tutoring is offered. Learners can contact the faculty member by telephone at no charge and by e-mail. Usually, learners who remain one year in a regional campus and then transfer to the main campus have developed greater abilities to use technology.

THE SECOND WAVE: MOBILE COMPUTING

In our academic mobile computing model, learners and faculty are equipped with laptop computers to enhance the learning process. Since Collège Boréal piloted its initial mobile computing project in September 1997, the scope of the program evolved from approximately 200 learners in four academic programs in the beginning to more than 1,200 learners, covering at one point in time close to 75% of the college's academic programs.

Unlike many institutions that have adopted mobile computing, Collège Boréal chose not to implement mobile computing in 100% of its programs. In fact, it deliberately scaled back the program for instructional and strategic reasons, as explained later. This evolution is the result of a highly structured approach in the training and support of faculty and learners, as well as a strong emphasis on technological development geared to enhancing and promoting educational innovation based on the humanistic model presented previously.

Many institutions were consulted before Collège Boréal decided to launch this initiative and it was discovered that although mobile computing had been implemented in many other places, there was no program anywhere operating with similar conditions and variables. Faculty, management, and learners had to work together to develop a suitable framework.

The Faculty Perspective

To make the mobile computing model feasible throughout most of the college's programs, a crucial step in the beginning was to develop an information technology culture and ensure the faculty's total immersion in it. This was accomplished in phases, beginning with a small team of pioneers leading up to the mainstream implementation.

In the spring of 1997, four programs were identified as pilot programs for the upcoming school year. Shortly after, all faculty members involved in these programs were given their first laptop computer, an IBM ThinkPad[J]. Other faculty members were encouraged to submit innovative educational or re-search-based project proposals related to the integration of this technology into the learning process. Those whose submissions were accepted also received a ThinkPad[J] computer. In total, close to 40 computers were given to faculty that spring. This provided four to six months of preparation time before the first learners entered the program in September. At this point, the support system was mainly among peers since most of these faculty members were already quite comfortable with computers and eager to learn more. Workshops were offered covering various software packages; IBM also sponsored presentations dealing with the use of technology in education.

A serious concern at this point was how to deal with faculty who were not quite as computer literate as the team of pioneers. Although their programs were not involved in the project for the 1997–1998 academic year, it was important to ensure that they would be adequately prepared for the following year, when most of Boréal's academic programs would include mobile comput-ing. The first step was to provide every full-time faculty member with his or her own laptop computer, which was done in October 1997. The next step was to develop a method of ensuring the mastery of basic computer skills. A study of the practices at other educational institutions followed by negotiations be-tween union and management led to a peer tutoring approach, known as "tech-coaching." In this model, a team of tech-coaches was identified among faculty, mostly from the group of pioneers. They each had six hours per week dedicated for this purpose in their workload form, which was equivalent to 96 hours throughout the semester to act as trainers to a group of faculty. In the same manner, members receiving the training were given three hours per week for one semester, or 48 hours, to participate in the weekly sessions. The ratio was usually one trainer to four trainees. This program lasted for the full 1997-1998 school year, and every member of faculty went through it. By the end of that year everyone was able to use a computer to some degree, from basic word processing and Internet searches to more advanced uses such as Web-page design and multimedia presentations.

Of course, knowing how to use a computer is not equivalent to knowing how to use a computer as a learning tool. In January 1998, still in the pilot year, *La Cuisine* (literally translated as "The Kitchen") was launched. Its purpose was to provide a center where faculty could gather to develop and share new skills and approaches to facilitate the integration of various technologies into the learning process. It also provided access to a variety of multimedia tools such as a high-end scanner, digital still and video cameras, as well as video editing equipment. *La Cuisine* was staffed by a full-time coordinator, a faculty member seconded for the semester. With the title of Instructional Designer, his responsibilities included one-on-one, on-demand training sessions with faculty, organizing and offering various workshops focusing on the educational aspects of technology, and researching the various trends and resources available in other institutions. Another initiative to aid with instructional design was the creation of a course called "Multimedia Applications." This course teamed up faculty members with learners to develop multimedia-based learning tools, using the tools and resources available from *La Cuisine*.

Until this stage, the focus had been on four pilot programs and preparation of faculty for the next step. In September 1998, mobile computing went from a project stage to a full-scale implementation. Although the aim was integration into 100% of postsecondary programs, faculty concerns about the impact on enrollment and the appropriateness of integration into certain programs warranted a reevaluation of the short-term plan. It is now a commonly held opinion among faculty that the college rushed into this initiative without having properly analyzed and calculated its impact, resulting in more negative than positive reactions in the first few months of the project. The project was able to go on despite this because of the dedication of the people involved, including faculty, management, and learners, resulting in 75% of first-year postsecondary programs "going mobile."

With this increase in mobile computing, the needs of faculty also evolved. Because everyone had attained at least a basic computer competency, the emphasis was now on actual classroom applications of technology. The tech-coaching program had served its purpose and was replaced with the "resource person" model. Four full-time faculty members were identified, one in each of the college's four schools: Technology and Natural Sciences, Business and Office Administration, Health Sciences, and Human Sciences. The six regional campuses also shared the equivalent of one full-time faculty position for this role. They were relieved of their teaching duties in order to assist their colleagues in their instructional development initiatives. Their duties were similar to those of the coordinator of *La Cuisine*, but with a more individualized approach. They handled much of the troubleshooting for the less experienced staff and guided many course material development projects in cooperation with *La Cuisine*. They went out of their way to identify and approach colleagues who were struggling and encourage the ones who were progressing.

In addition to the five "resource person" positions and the coordinator of *La Cuisine*, the 1998–1999 academic year saw the appointment of a full-time project coordinator, a temporary administrative position created to oversee the implementation of the overall strategic plan governing the mobile computing program. This person was again a faculty member seconded to focus his efforts on this initiative. This brought the faculty support team up to seven full-time positions.

Now in its third year of full implementation, Collège Boréal has the majority of both its first- and second-year postsecondary programs "running mobile." At this stage, the support needs have again changed. With most faculty members having at least one year of experience with this approach, the number of support people was dropped to two faculty members sharing one full position in *La Cuisine*. Also, the position of Mobile Computing Project Co-ordinator was eliminated and the associated responsibilities were distributed among the existing administrative staff. It is no longer considered a project. Instead, it has become a part of the information technology culture that permeates and partially defines Collège Boréal.

At this time, the mobile computing initiative includes approximately 115 full-time faculty, as well as a multitude of part-time members. It is a part of 50 postsecondary programs out of a possible 62 postsecondary programs. There are at least as many different approaches to the actual implementation of the laptop computer and other technologies into the learning process as there are people involved, since everyone has his or her own personal perspective. Classroom uses range from simple Internet searches to advanced Web-page design, from a simple communication tool to the control of complicated electronic circuits with programmable logic controllers.

The impact on teaching has been significant. Some teachers report increased preparation time due to the development of new tools, such as Web pages or electronic presentations while others claim a diminished workload because of the ready availability of resources. Some say that they were able to cover 40% more material in a semester with access to technology while others covered less material than in previous years due to technical problems encountered in class. It is still too early to provide an accurate conclusion as to the type of impact technology has on teaching. However, the overall results up to this time seem quite promising.

The Learner Perspective

Although mobile computing and other classroom technologies always seem driven by faculty and administration, it is important to remember that the

ultimate goal of these initiatives is to significantly enhance the learning experience for the learners. Accordingly, a support structure needed to be implemented for them in much the same way as for the faculty. Without these
mechanisms, not only would the learner's chance of success be compromised,
but the job of faculty would be much more difficult since learners would
continuously look to them for technical support.

In the pilot year, support was provided in a variety of ways, most of them
informal. The main formal structure was the creation of the CTIC (*Centre des
technologies de l'information et de la communication*—Centre for Information and
Communication Technologies). The CTIC consisted mainly of one full-time
technician to provide full technical support during regular business hours and a
team of student monitors providing support in the evenings and on the
weekends. The technician shared space with *La Cuisine*. Their room opened
onto a large open work area filled with modular workstations, belonging to the
mobile computing learners. They gathered here to work on their assignments or
pass the time playing network games or surfing the Internet. This area also
provided the main informal support mechanism by fostering an atmosphere of
peers helping peers. Finally, because this was at the pilot stage, the faculty
associated with the project spent a lot of time helping their learners overcome
the different challenges they faced.

In the first year of the full implementation, the CTIC evolved to a staff of
three full-time technicians, occupying their own room while *La Cuisine* moved
into the room next door, both of them remaining linked to the learner's open
work area. The result was that all technical support for both learners and
faculty could be found in one space. A side effect of this grouping of services
was to encourage mingling and sharing of expertise between learners and
faculty, since they often shared the same problems and challenges with their
computers.

Of course, all this technical support would not go very far without a sound
computer skills training strategy. Learners begin their training from the moment they receive their laptop computers. A three- to four-hour session when
computers are distributed is mandatory, in which the basics of the laptop itself
are covered, such as the location of the power switch and proper battery
charging procedures as well as basic operating system commands, such as the
proper shut-down procedure before turning the power off.

In the pilot year and the first year of full implementation, learners received a
compulsory 10-hour introductory computer training course at the beginning of
the semester. These sessions dealt with the care of a laptop computer, basic
operating system commands, virus protection, e-mail, Internet, and the use of
the college's internal computer network. Additional training was available
through college-funded peer tutoring programs as well as the availability of
one-on-one training sessions throughout the semester. In the following year,

these 10-hour sessions were dropped in favor of a 48-hour credit course spread over the first semester, three hours per week, in order to provide a structured, ongoing training mechanism.

The first year of full implementation saw the addition of in-class support through a group of learners known as *étoiles informatiques* or Computer Stars. The Stars received peer counseling training and were identified in the first few weeks by wearing a badge in class. This showed their classmates that they were available and willing to answer the routine questions that could come up during class time, such as saving or printing documents. Although well structured, this program was dropped for the 1999–2000 school year because it was considered unnecessary. There were always a few learners in each group willing to do this without the framework provided by the Stars program.

Mobile computing obviously carries a heavy cost. The strategy adopted at Collège Boréal was to have the learners pay a technology fee of $1,200 per academic year. This fee gave them access to a laptop computer and all the college's computer network resources, any software packages required for their course of study, free technical support, home Internet access, and insurance against theft and accidental damage. The actual cost of the program was much higher per learner than $1,200, but the college felt that a higher cost would be prohibitive to many of our incoming learners and therefore decided to subsidize the cost to a certain extent.

The impact on the learning process for these learners is significant. They now have access to an immeasurable wealth of resources and information in the classroom, at their fingertips through their laptop computers. Many repetitive and time-consuming tasks are eliminated, leaving more time for actual learning experiences. Outside the classroom, they have access to the same resources as inside the classroom. They also have a simple means of communicating with their teachers and classmates through e-mail or electronic discussion groups.

This same tool also provides a significant source of distraction for many learners through readily available chat lines, music, and games, not to mention adult-oriented materials inappropriate within a classroom. These circumstances necessitate an adaptation both from the learner's and the teacher's perspective. A learner who gives in to these distractions during class runs a higher risk of failing since he or she is missing out on important classroom activities. A teacher must modify his or her teaching strategies to minimize the opportunities for learners to stray in class and must constantly monitor learner activities during computer-oriented activities.

Many learners find all the technology overwhelming for the first few weeks, but as the semester progresses, they learn to tame it. Others recognize the power and potential of the tool immediately, both for work and pleasure. Eventually, most of the learners say they could not live without their laptop.

The Technological Perspective

For an effective mobile computing program in an academic setting, a strong technological infrastructure is an obvious requirement. With this in mind, the main campus of the college was built with approximately 2,400 network connections, or "drops," mostly in classrooms, but also in the library, the cafeteria, and even the pub, allowing for maximum connectivity. The other six campuses are also similarly equipped. The network structure was designed using state-of-the-art components in order to accommodate this high level of network traffic.

Most of the classrooms are equipped with data projectors and sound systems to facilitate the presentation of electronic material, as well as document cameras. Because ergonomics are always an issue with long-term computer use, the classrooms are also equipped with office-quality chairs that allow adjustment of the back and seat height. These room configurations allow both learners and faculty to maximize the effectiveness of the technological tools in enhancing the learning experience.

Mobile Computing Today

Mobile computing programs are appearing in more and more educational institutions because of the valuable advantages added to the learning experience. Although it is still too early to form an accurate evaluation of the program's success for Collège Boréal, it is being closely monitored. For example, some of the issues relating to the attitudes and perceptions toward mobile computing are currently being addressed in an independent three-year study conducted by the Ontario Institute for Studies in Education at the University of Toronto.

Mobile Computing Update

However, after three years of experience with mobile computing, more recently concerns about enrollment, costs, and maintaining overall program quality have led to significant developments in Collège Boréal's mobile computing program.

The most visible change was the cost to the learner. Although the technological fee of $1200 that learners were required to pay to participate in this program was already the lowest among the Ontario colleges, many members of the college community feared that this cost could still be a deterrent from enrollment. In response to this concern, a committee was created in September 1999 to identify strategies to reduce this fee. The consultations involved faculty, administration, and learners, and resulted in a 37% reduction in the mandatory fee for the learners, to $750, effective in September 2000. The only significant loss of service with this reduction was the elimination of Internet access from home. It was noted that many of our incoming learners already had Internet accounts at home and this resulted in a duplication of services. Another approach was the implementation of an equipment fee of $150 that all learners at the college pay as part of their incidental fees. This fee covers the costs of the information technology infrastructure that all learners share, whether or not they are part of the mobile computing program. The balance of the reduction was achieved mainly by being vigilant with software purchases and our choice of technologies. The option to "rent to own" a laptop computer was also made available for the first time, in response to learner requests.

The other main development was the result of a more complicated process. In the early fall of 1999, the faculty union held a general assembly to identify its members' priorities regarding the general evolution of the college, with a common goal of increasing enrollment and overall academic program quality. The strongest recommendation to come out of this meeting was the request for a reevaluation of the mobile computing initiative—specifically, to look at removing some academic programs from this approach. This was in sharp contrast to the often repeated goal by the college administration of 100% program participation by the year 2000. After some negotiations, the administration agreed that it was time for a reevaluation since Collège Boréal was now in its second year (and its third for certain programs) of experience with mobile computing.

Although the initiation of this last process was quite difficult at times, once the faculty and the administration agreed to the goals and methods of the reevaluation process, things generally went smoothly. A survey was administered to faculty regarding the amount of in-class utilization of the laptop computers, by academic program. This, along with consultations, led to the identification of programs in which the use of computers adapted very well to the learning process, resulting in their actual integration as an in-class learning tool. These programs remained in the mobile computing program, meaning that the computer is a mandatory tool for the learners. Other programs showed less of an adaptability for in-class learning for various reasons. Learners enrolling in these programs were therefore not required to obtain a laptop computer. This was not to say that the laptop computer was not a powerful learning tool for these learners. It was simply saying that in-class use was insufficient to warrant making it required. In keeping with the belief that this tool provides learners with a great deal of benefits, learners enrolling in "nonmobile" programs will still have the option of paying the same technological fee and obtaining the same services as the learners enrolling in the "mobile" programs. In September 2000, just over half of Collège Boréal's academic programs participated in the mobile computing initiative.

To succeed, an initiative such as our mobile computing program must be in a constant state of evolution and reevaluation. As the available technologies change and the job market evolves, Collège Boréal will face new demands as well as new opportunities. Programs like mobile computing need to be constantly monitored and adapted and everyone involved in their success must work together.

THE THIRD WAVE: ONLINE LEARNING

Collège Boréal is presently applying the experience acquired in videoconferencing and mobile computing to deploy a comprehensive online learning strategy. Without even formulating a specific direction for online learning, faculty have inadvertently been using some of the tools and strategies observed in other postsecondary online initiatives.

In December 1999, a scan of online teaching and learning activities in Ontario college and university systems revealed that online learning definitions include one or more of the following elements :

- Delivery and management of learning using intranet and Internet resources, with or without a face-to-face component.
- Electronic distribution of course materials, text based as well as multimedia.
- Use of electronic communication tools such as e-mail, discussion groups, and chat rooms.

Online learning involves the use of learning technologies. The Council of Ontario Universities has defined these tools as: "Those information and technology tools that provide increased opportunities for interaction with learning materials and among learners, as designed and guided by faculty" (Council of Ontario Universities, 2000). This definition implies that a course may be, entirely or in part, facilitated with Internet or intranet tools as per learning outcome requirements. It is observed in both colleges and universities that learning technologies are not limited to courses entirely facilitated online. Face-to-face and videoconferencing courses also integrate learning technologies based on the advantages they provide.

A survey on the use of WebCT, a popular online learning technology, in Ontario colleges and universities was conducted in February and March 2000. The results indicate that 87% of WebCT-based courses currently in use or under development are for on-campus applications (Danielson, 2000). This implies that face-to-face courses are being enhanced with online learning technologies. For practical purposes, the definition of online learning is not limited to the realm of distance education.

With this in mind, Collège Boréal has been active in the field of online learning with its mobile computing initiative. For example, a tool such as the Windows Network Neighborhood™ share is widely used for course material distribution. Faculty regularly use Lotus Notes™ for e-mail and discussion groups to facilitate exchanges both within and between campuses. Learners and faculty frequently use the internet as teaching and learning resources. The library subscribes to over 2,000 publications online which are in turn available to the college population.

Most existing online activities at Collège Boréal are related to the integration of mobile computing. Both synchronous and asynchronous learning activities that make use of Web-based technologies are currently used by a number of faculty members. Most of this use is derived from the training received from the tech-coaches and resource persons. Standards have yet to be developed for comprehensive online learning activities.

The faculty support and development strategy must evolve as further tools are being considered to adapt specific courses for use completely online or to enhance the existing online component of "hybrid" courses. Lotus LearningSpace™ and WebCT™ are being evaluated as potential standard platforms. Selection of such tools will orient the evolution of online learning to courses delivered entirely over the Internet.

Past experience has shown that faculty support is critical in successful implementation of technologies. This facet is not lost in the development of a comprehensive online strategy. A team of five experts has been assembled from academics, learner support, registrar services, administration, and marketing to define the future directions of online teaching and learning at Collège Boréal. This team worked from May 1999 to March 2000 to research and define the best practices and directions in online learning while exploring the possibilities of corporate partnerships. As a result, an integrated team for multimedia production and faculty support has been established. This team and its approach is known as bore@l.edu. Expertise in instructional design and teaching, multimedia and graphic design, Internet content development and management, programming and server management, administration and marketing will form the core competencies of bore@l.edu. Content expertise and specific consultant services will be retained based on project requirements through faculty and/or corporate partner and customer involvement.

Bore@l.edu will have five main roles :

1. Plan and develop courses.
2. Standardize online course development and management through selection and use of technologies.
3. Provide faculty support and training in selection and use of online course tools.
4. Participate in strategic planning for learner and faculty support.
5. Research market opportunities and establish partnerships.

Bore@l.edu will promote a standard interdisciplinary approach to specific course development projects. The team will provide the human and technical resources that ensure standards in the development and management of online learning. As a complementary strategy to diversify the types of learning opportunities, partnerships are encouraged.

Part of bore@l.edu's role is to identify training niches, develop marketing plans, and sell the products and services available online. Course delivery can only occur if learners enroll.

Learners may be individuals seeking specific training, while a majority of learners may come from training agreements negotiated with employers who wish to provide a range of courses to their employees as part of a professional development package. Marketing targets both the academic and corporate sectors.

As part of this strategy, bore@l.edu has signed a partnership with VUSME (Virtual University for Small and Medium Enterprise) for exclusive resale rights in Canada of French language online courses in E-commerce and Entrepreneurship. These courses have been successfully integrated in the college curriculum and have also been purchased by businesses. Collège Boréal has also negotiated reseller rights of the English versions of the courses throughout northeastern Ontario. With this strategy, Collège Boréal can offer a variety of certificates easily customized to meet business and program needs. Partnerships such as this one are continuously being researched and evaluated.

Collège Boréal continues its integration of learning technologies for online learning. A multidisciplinary team will be hired to head the implementation of a course development center. Furthermore, a consultation process held in August and September 2000 has gathered ideas and recommendations from the college population. The report identifies goals and challenges along with leads on best practices and resources necessary to ensure the successful development of online learning within a realistic time frame. Furthermore, the report provides an opportunity for stakeholder input recognition as well as initial buy-in and confidence building.

The recommendations are grouped by themes on teaching and learning, infrastructure, finances, planning, and other. Each area is being addressed through the development of action plans for design and implementation. Work groups on student retention, model and philosophy development, and technology testing and selection have a basic framework from which to begin. Interrelations between the working groups will provide an integrated approach to implementing a broad-scale e-learning strategy.

A production center for faculty support in the development of online learning initiatives has been launched in September. This center deals with the instructional design issues and project management for electronic course development. What is most important, dedicated personnel can concentrate on the issues pertaining to e-learning.

LESSONS LEARNED

As part of any large-scale initiative such as the ubiquitous integration of learning technologies in an educational setting, the first element that is required is a clear vision. Collège Boréal has articulated at the outset that its survival depended on the use of technologies such as videoconferencing and audioconferencing. The technological focus continued with the integration of mobile computing. The element that must be retained in the planning process is that any technology use must hinge on appropriate teaching and learning strategies.

Collège Boréal has learned that it is important to invest in professional development, specifically regarding the use of technologies. Technical support, mentoring, and tech-coaching prove to be efficient mechanisms that focus on the technical aspects of using technologies as teaching tools. The necessary resources must be made available to use the tools appropriately.

What happens in a first phase is that the focus is on the tools and the teaching strategies. It is not as obvious or easy to focus on learning strategies adapted to the learners and their future employment requirements. Further resources must be invested in defining these directions. As the learner population diversifies, its profile should include a demographic assessment along with its expectations and future needs. This will focus where and how technologies are to be integrated and used in teaching and learning. Faculty support should be adjusted according to these elements.

A strong planning process is a must and should include the following elements:

1. Definition of the institution's vision, objectives, and expectations.
2. Communication of the vision, objectives, and expectations.
3. Adoption and buy-in by faculty through open discussion and negotiation.
4. Tracking and assessment of past experience to learn and evolve from the results with respect to the orientations set initially.

Faculty support is not only a strategy that relates to teaching and technology use but is also a process of defining learning needs and adapting teaching and learning strategies according to expectations and needs. Faculty buy-in remains an important challenge to be met in the broad adoption of teaching and learning technologies.

FUTURE DIRECTIONS

Collège Boréal has set out in its vision to be "innovative and bold through the use of evolving and proactive strategies centered on the needs and expectations of their diversifying clientele." The college also "recognizes the value and the importance of the role to be played by each member of its community," including faculty, administration, support staff, and learners along with community stakeholders.

Future initiatives have to be developed based on the assessment of the lessons learned. Many changes have occurred in the last five years that prepare us for new ones. A process that includes all members is critical. Each person must understand the ramifications of the vision and adopt it as the guiding principle. The process must instill stability while remaining dynamic.

Among the strategies that can be identified at the present time, a comprehensive professional development plan is to be redefined in light of the ever-changing situation. This plan should guarantee that all members of the college community not only follow basic information technology (IT) courses but can apply the knowledge, skills, and competencies in teaching, learning, and everyday work situations. The plan should also include incentives and mechanisms that allow early adopters and advanced IT users to move ahead to develop new working examples of successful strategies.

The faculty development plan should be based on the needs and expectations of the clientele, namely, the learners. A process that tracks institutional progress within the scope of these parameters should be in place to justify both the success and the consequences of straying from these objectives. The assessment and improvement of the system are an integral part of the process.

Future directions in innovation are to be taken on a road that remains to be built. Developing a process and strategies that foster success requires a clear vision, a communication plan, and well-defined roles. The focus is to be on recognition of success, lessons learned, and the continuous goal of equipping teachers and learners with the tools and strategies to meet their evolving needs and expectations.

REFERENCES

Council of Ontario Universities. (2000). *A Time To Sow: Report from the Task Force on Learning Technologies.* COU.671. www.cou.on.ca.
Danielson, Richard, R. (2000). Ontario WebCT Consortium Usage Statistics—January 2000. Laurentian University. http://webct.laurentian.ca/webct/onstatjan_2000.htm.

CHAPTER 5

Designing Advanced Learning Communities
Virginia Tech's Story

Anne H. Moore

INTRODUCTION

Colleges and universities are integrating technology in teaching and learning as a result of numerous forces. One impetus is to fill the well-publicized void of "knowledge workers" for business and industry and to help provide a foundation for advanced learning in a knowledge-based economy. The cost of higher education also has been a major concern in many arenas during the 1990s. This has been accompanied by a heightened interest in the affordability of using technology in instruction, the quality of the results, and a pressure to show productivity gains in teaching and learning.

In a 1998 report of the National Learning Infrastructure Initiative (NLII), Carol Twigg said that academic productivity is at the forefront of higher education's consciousness, creating a pressing need for institutions to go beyond theory and show results. To move toward beneficial results, she suggested that three areas of activity are needed: (1) to spotlight efforts to redesign learning environments; (2) to develop new tools to assist reengineering; and (3) to develop more models of productive learning environments (NLII Meeting Notes, June 1998). As an example of redesigning learning environments, Twigg described a new initiative at Virginia Tech—the Math Emporium—which offers mathematics courses in a 24 x 7 computer-based learning environment to more than 7,000 students each semester. Although spotlighting efforts like the Math Emporium is useful, the complete institutional environment of these prototypes needs to be taken into consideration for this information to be beneficial to others. Such frontline, programmatic initiatives usually spring from particular circumstances and supporting infrastructures.

The impetus for Virginia Tech to build a faculty development infrastructure that would ultimately lead to launching such a large-scale project as the Math Emporium can be traced to the early 1990s when the Commonwealth of Virginia experienced a recession. To cope with shrinking resources, Virginia's Governor and General Assembly called for the state's public colleges and universities to restructure. Charged with serving more students with fewer resources from the state, Virginia Tech decided to attempt to build institutional capacity using technology.

This chapter will illuminate that effort, using Carol Twigg's three arenas of activity to help delineate the elements of Virginia Tech's emergent progress. This faculty development case will show how the three essential elements—redesigned learning environments, new tools to assist reengineering, and multiple models of productive learning environments—figure as integral parts of a developing infrastructure and its evolving results at Virginia Tech.

BACKGROUND: VIRGINIA POLYTECHNIC INSTITUTE AND STATE UNIVERSITY

Founded in 1872, Virginia Tech is a comprehensive land-grant institution located in Blacksburg, Virginia. This Research I university is the largest in the commonwealth and has over 1,500 faculty, 25,000 students in eight colleges, and 160,000 alumni scattered across the globe. Its College of Arts and Sciences is the largest college on campus. It is also the largest arts and sciences college in the state, as is the university's College of Engineering. Ranked among the top 50 research universities in the nation with numerous highly ranked programs, the university offers approximately 70 bachelor's degree programs and 120 master's and doctoral programs. In cooperation with Virginia State University, Virginia Tech jointly operates Virginia Cooperative Extension (VCE). VCE's mission calls for the two universities to extend their learning communities to over 100 local extension offices and to six 4-H centers across the state. In addition, Virginia Tech has five education centers, some of which are operated jointly with other Virginia institutions, and research and experiment stations in targeted regions across the state.

INSTRUCTIONAL DEVELOPMENT INITIATIVE

Because Virginia Tech already had a robust technological infrastructure in place in the early 1990s, with many students already using computers extensively in their studies, the university wanted to encourage its faculty to make as full use as possible of existing tools to improve student learning and access to materials. This approach to state-mandated restructuring proved to be a significant strategic decision. Indeed, Carol Twiggs's second area of necessary activity in this area is to provide new tools to assist those wishing to reengineer courses and programs. Thus, in 1993, Virginia Tech attempted to create just such an infrastructure through an Instructional Development Initiative (IDI). The first "tools" that developed included several organizations and incentive programs within the university designed to focus on faculty development and technology-assisted instruction. Later, with the growth of a competitive vendor market in learning management systems, other more technology-based instructional tools became available and were incorporated systematically into development efforts across the university.

Virginia Tech's answer to the recession-driven call to restructure from Virginia's State Council of Higher Education and General Assembly was unique in the state. Its provost and chief information officer, in particular, analyzed ways to use existing resources, like equipment, software, and advanced networks, more effectively to improve teaching and learning. Then as now, another external force pressuring the university to respond came from businesses that were asking institutions to step up to the technology needs of the workforce. Ultimately, the university decided to redistribute internal operating funds and Equipment Trust Fund monies (funds allocated by the state especially for equipment purchases) and to focus defined development efforts on teaching. In launching the Instructional Development Initiative in 1993, the university reallocated 1.5 percent from its base budget and immediately redirected that support to instruction. Later, when the university formally updated its strategic plan in 1996, it formalized its resolve to sustain comprehensive instructional development by stating that these initiatives were to be faculty-driven, to include all faculty, and to respond to citizens' needs for more flexible access to education over a lifetime.

The premier initiative, IDI, was designed to accomplish three things: (1) outfit classrooms and laboratories so that faculty can use technology in distributed instruction; (2) establish origination sites so that faculty can deliver instruction at a distance; and (3) organize and maintain the Faculty Development Institute (FDI).

The Faculty Development Institute assists faculty in learning how to use technology in teaching, and has emerged as pivotal to the university's success in this arena. In its efforts to expand institutional capacity using the FDI as a vehicle, the university has assumed that three compelling questions need to inform the evolving process: (1) how faculty can best use instructional technology to improve their teaching; (2) what the impact of this technology is on student learning that occurs in various settings and under many conditions; and (3) how the interaction between faculty and students will drive discovery.

The FDI is designed as a four-year recurring program that will help all Virginia Tech faculty members learn how to integrate technology into their instruction through an intensive workshop environment. The workshop programs have evolved over time. At the beginning, a conscious effort was made to target faculty who taught core curriculum courses and were least likely to have access to current technology. Faculty from the College of Arts and Sciences made up the majority of early participants. One of the incentives to attend FDI is a new desktop computer, an Ethernet/Internet connection, a standardized package of software, and ongoing support. The FDI is also used as a way to establish an equipment and software replacement cycle for faculty.

In a typical week during the summer, two-day, three-day, and four-day workshops are conducted concurrently. Typically, there are two to four groups per week with 20 people in each group. Faculty are assigned so that groups will have mixed technological ability and participants will be from mixed academic departments. During the workshops, an online evaluation is conducted every 90 minutes for quality assurance. Faculty apply what they are learning by developing a personal project throughout the workshop. They receive brief presentations or demonstrations followed by coaching, if needed, from graduate assistants (one for every four faculty) and other paid professionals, some of whom are faculty colleagues. In the workshops faculty learn to integrate a range of technologies into their projects, from Web-based to video-based to CD-ROMs, depending on the instructional goals they aim to achieve.

Over time, successful workshops have illuminated a few practical points about working successfully with faculty:

1. Do not overload participants with information and keep the information practical, especially at first.
2. Make sure that there are many opportunities—not just in summer—to learn, to discuss, and to get help.
3. Respect the level of knowledge participants have about technology and about teaching and help them build on what they know.
4. Keep the emphasis on practical issues of teaching and learning and not on technology.
5. Help participants think about the definition of success for a project from the start, in terms of changing their teaching and in terms of how or what students will learn.
6. Use faculty as mentors.
7. Focus on the long-term development of people by building rapport, trust, and credibility.
8. Do not introduce new technologies that people cannot access or use.

Changes in the FDI curriculum occur on an annual cycle because of the rapid rate of technological change and the evolving sophistication of faculty in using technology. The changes are based on faculty requests received as part of an annual survey of participants slotted for workshops. FDI has a common thread emphasizing the practical application of technology in teaching. In 1998, a workshop track was added in which participants learned about instructional design principles and student learning.

At the end of the first four-year cycle in 1996, 96% of Virginia Tech's faculty had attended the institute's workshops and seminars. As for distributed and distance learning physical infrastructure, over 50 presentation classrooms and 13 origination sites were established during the first four-year phase; computer laboratories now exist in strategic places across campus that serve students' needs for accessibility to modern instructional resources. The $10 million price tag for the first four-year cycle was largely for equipment and software, since full-time FDI staff have numbered less than 10 in any given year.

In the summer of 1999, over 400 faculty participated in FDI's three-day summer workshops, in the second year of the institute's second cycle. In addition to the summer workshops, approximately 75 "just-in-time" workshops are available during each academic year to faculty on topics that they often request. Furthermore, the university has successfully extended this mature professional development model to K–12 teachers who need either certification in instructional technology or want a Master's degree in Instructional Technology. Elementary and secondary school teachers may receive training, certification, or a degree through Virginia Tech's College of Human Resources and Education, whose faculty and graduate students have also played key roles in the ever-evolving Faculty Development Institute. Where the FDI began with such workshops as Using Your Computer and How to Use PowerPoint, today's programming includes instruction on using Geographic Information Systems (GIS), applying streaming audio and video technologies in teaching, and more. Faculty who are proficient in using technology now often participate as coaches for their colleagues in FDI in summer workshops and year-round, occasional seminars.

The success of the Faculty Development Institute has resulted in several conclusions for the university:

- First, despite popular opinion, faculty do not resist the use of technology when given the resources and support to understand it and to use it to improve their teaching.
- Second, technology can be used effectively to improve teaching in all disciplines and by faculty with varying degrees of technological sophistication.
- Third, faculty support must be easily accessible, ongoing, and escalated in sophistication as faculty seek new and better approaches to incorporating technology in the classroom.

The Faculty Development Institute received a prestigious, national Theodore Hesburgh award in 1998 in recognition of the quality and comprehensiveness of this four-year, cycling faculty development effort. In that same year, the institute was also singled out by the American Productivity and Quality Center (APQC) and the State Higher Education Executive Officers (SHEEO) benchmarking study as one of five North American Best Practices institutions in assisting faculty to use technology in the classroom.

EFFECTS OF THE FACULTY DEVELOPMENT INSTITUTE

There are numerous spin-off effects of having more than a critical mass of faculty with sophisticated knowledge of technology in teaching. Virginia Tech's Cyberschool, a voluntary collection of faculty who seek to assist each other in integrating technology in teaching, numbers over 60 members who have created over 350 courses, all or a portion of which are online. A recent Cyberschool initiative involved an Online Summer School in 1998 and 1999 that reached over 500 students each summer across Virginia and beyond. The continued growth in Virginia Tech's summer school enrollments tentatively validates the university's theory that it can serve its own students better through a distributed learning environment in summer, since most of them return to their homes to work during these months. This also offers students a means of accelerating their studies, if they wish.

These successful summer school efforts were continued through fall and spring semesters of the 1998–1999 and 1999–2000 academic years in a pilot program aimed at making access to instruction at Virginia Tech more flexible and transparent for residential students. To realize these aims fully, such instructional initiatives must be successfully integrated with electronic administrative information systems. Then students will have access to electronically enhanced teaching, advising, testing, and advanced communications as well as admissions, registration, financial operations, and other administrative necessities. Virginia Tech is actively engaged in making this kind of administration transparent to students and an asset to faculty, staff, and student transactions and communication. With such integrated systems in place, more students can be served incrementally at a fraction of the costs associated with student enrollment growth in the past, with better information sharing and management.

With access, quality, and cost in mind, the university next created the Center for Innovation in Learning to provide grants to faculty to develop courseware in strategic, high-priority, curricular areas. Although the FDI is more of a grassroots faculty development initiative, this center is designed to provide structure for selected programming. To date, over 100 grants totaling more that $2 million have been awarded to faculty whose projects are focused on redesigning instruction in high demand areas—core curriculum courses, upper level courses, distance learning programs, and modular instructional segments. The center is conducting feasibility studies to ascertain demand in particular content areas and is assessing the effectiveness of all its efforts. The center also presents annual awards to recognize faculty who have made outstanding contributions to the integration of technology in teaching and learning. Award winners agree to demonstrate their exceptional practices to colleagues in seminars or workshops, as needed.

In spring 1999, the university established the Institute for Distance and Distributed Learning to solidify and support the diffusion of innovation in this arena. With 12 graduate and professional programs offered at a distance and many undergraduate courses and noncredit offerings available in a distributed learning environment, this newest institute is a vital piece of the learning infrastructure. The institute's advisory committee has representatives from each of the university's eight colleges, whose charge is to develop policies and procedures for the support of distance and distributed learning at Virginia Tech and to help coordinate instructional development efforts across the university.

Finally, unexpected synergies have occurred as a result of extending the university's faculty development activities across types of organizations and institutions. For example, as a result of summer workshops with one urban Virginia school district, the university and that district—Falls Church Public Schools—formed a partnership to create the Technology Learning Center in Falls Church. (Falls Church is located in northern Virginia; Virginia Tech's main campus is 250 miles away in southwest Virginia.) By jointly renovating an unused pod at the George Mason Middle School and High School complex, which stands next to the Virginia Tech/University of Virginia Center in northern Virginia, the school system and university are able to use modernized space efficiently to offer technology-assisted instruction during the day to school students and teacher training in technology-assisted instruction in the evening and on weekends. The Technology Learning Center also links to other sites across the commonwealth on Net.Work.Virginia, the statewide, broadband, IP/ATM network, which is managed by Virginia Tech.

PRODUCTIVE LEARNING ENVIRONMENTS

Twigg's third area of suggested activity is to create additional or multiple models of more productive learning environments, models that assist faculty and institutions in breaking out of familiar, yet less productive instructional molds, and in creating new ways to learn. With multiple models from which to choose, faculty have more visible options as they seek to create their own new learning environments. This essential activity focuses on stimulating the creation of a breadth of technology-assisted approaches to productive learning, an activity that also assists an institution in having a critical mass of faculty engaged in experimental instructional efforts across many areas of study. The

Center for Innovation in Learning seeds such activities at Virginia Tech and also lobbies for appropriate structural support of successful new models.

For example, the Dean of the College of Arts and Sciences, who also sits on the center's advisory board, has included goals in his college's strategic plan for rewarding faculty in promotion and tenure reviews for their efforts in creating new distributed and distance learning environments. In addition, Arts and Sciences faculty have created a Chemistry Learning Center, an innovative learning environment for improving students' performance in "killer courses"; offered Emerging Scholars Program (ESP) calculus that has improved the grades of at-risk mathematics students; and developed online Java-based worksheets in economics as well as supply and demand exercises and simulated markets to aid student learning. Likewise, collaboration between faculty and students in engineering and business has resulted in the creation of a Virtual Corporation. Here, undergraduate students use the university's robust infrastructure (e.g., advanced telecommunications and computing facilities and support) to form teams that design, develop, and produce a product or service for the marketplace, often in collaboration with an external industry partner.

THE MATH EMPORIUM

In this new, rapidly evolving environment, traditional approaches to delineating differences between instruction, infrastructure, and facilities often do not provide accurate descriptions or understandings of an activity, much less the kinds of learning taking place. For example, Virginia Tech's Math Emporium represents a significant reallocation of university resources to instruction, with seed funding from the Center for Innovation in Learning, that resulted in the first year of operation in being able to teach pre-calculus and linear algebra to more students with better learning results than before. The emporium's development involved the highly labor-intensive effort of at least 12 mathematics faculty to design the emporium, write the software and texts for the courses where it could not be purchased, and manage a 24 x 7 enterprise. The faculty have designed the new software to help students visualize the mathematics. They have also organized the learning in modules, so that students could easily return to specific mathematic concepts or transactions should they need to refresh their memory. These two courses remain high curricular priorities, since they are designed for first-year students who need a particular mathematical foundation prior to entering numerically intensive majors.

At the beginning of its third year of operation in 1999, the Math Emporium offered approximately 7,000 students per semester over 20 subjects in mathematics that they can pursue in an advanced learning community environment. The renovation of leased space near the university for this advanced learning community, with 500 dual platform workstations connected to

Net.Work.Virginia, staffed at peak hours by faculty who assist students one-on-one as they work at their own pace, is an integral part of the learning enterprise. Faculty are actively developing and migrating more topics in mathematics from the traditional classroom environment to the emporium and over 60 faculty currently participate in teaching emporium-based courses. In addition, emporium faculty have agreed to include high school students who wish to study mathematics at a distance and have begun pilot testing the effort. High school math teachers have participated in training programs in the emporium in the summers. It goes without saying that as much organizational learning goes on at the emporium and across the university, with all of is growth pangs, as student learning. The concept of technology laboratory turned advanced learning community is one that, at first, must be seen by some to be believed. Students of all ages approach learning differently, and faculty approach teaching differently.

VIRTUAL REALITY AT VIRGINIA TECH

Yet another noteworthy example of faculty ingenuity and application is the integration of CAVE Automated Virtual Environment (CAVE) applications in instruction. Virginia Tech's CAVE, which opened in winter 1998, allows faculty to create three-dimensional simulations and visualizations either in the three-dimensional space of a CAVE, or on the flat surface of an Immersadesk (the equivalent of one side of a CAVE), or on a wall. All eight colleges at Virginia Tech are supporting applications development in the CAVE, with students learning to develop the applications even as they are gaining knowledge of a content area. Architecture students can design buildings; design students create rooms; transportation students highways; entomology students the insides of a cockroach; molecular biology students genetic structures; humanities students the settings for narratives. Perhaps one of the best explanations of the teaching possibilities in a CAVE is a video produced by Virginia's Fairfax County Public School System encouraging K–12 teachers to experiment with this powerful new visualization tool in the schools by having Virginia Tech faculty demonstrate their newly developed teaching tools. Elementary and secondary teachers can, like their university faculty counterparts, create CAVE visualizations on their own computers and send them over the Internet to a nearby CAVE for their students to view by appointment.

ASSESSING NEW LEARNING ENVIRONMENTS

The results for students' learning are positive. Here is what Virginia Tech discovered in assessing biology courses (Sloan Foundation, ACCESS Project, 1995) that incorporated asynchronous instructional elements, including course

Web sites; online faculty "office hours;" electronic "chat rooms" with fellow students; and 24-hour network access to all class materials, including practice exams, lecture notes, and computer graphics of complex biology concepts presented in the classroom lecture.

1. Students reported that they had greater access to class materials, professors, and other students in these courses than in traditional classes. As a result, there was more student and faculty interaction as well as a team approach to learning.
2. Lecture notes posted on the course Web site allowed students to focus on learning rather than note taking, fostering a higher level of thinking and comprehension during class.
3. Students performed at—and in some cases above—the proficiency level of their peers in traditional lecture classes.
4. Students changed from passive to active learners—a development that some students had difficulty adjusting to at first. They found this kind of learning more demanding than simply continuing the I-talk-you-listen model they had known all their lives. But by the end of a course, students reported that they spent more time discovering information and learning on their own than they would have in a traditional class. Repeatedly, they said they were more motivated and eager to learn in these technology-enhanced courses, especially once they were familiar with the technology.

The university found similar results in unrelated studies in other disciplines. In a high-demand, core curriculum philosophy course, for example, student performance was shown to be better than that of their peers on 15 out of 16 criteria in an independent assessment of learning outcomes in the technologically enhanced instruction when compared to the outcomes of traditional instruction. In the Math Emporium, the percentage of students making satisfactory progress in and completing courses like pre-calculus and linear algebra has increased, while the failure rate has gone down. For example, in the first year after the emporium opened, the failure rate for linear algebra was down by 39 percent.

As mentioned earlier, the Center for Innovation in Learning is assessing all projects that it funds. The results are demonstrating the process and benefits of a hybrid quantitative-qualitative approach to assessment and its impact on future projects and policy at the university and beyond. The challenge of the assessment team is not only to report the progress and outcomes of each project, but also to establish a standard for judging effectiveness across projects. This involves using stated project objectives of formative and summative evaluation, and the well-known "Seven Principles of Good Practice in Undergraduate Education" (Chickering and Gamson, 1987) as a framework for comparison. In addition, the university purchased a site license for the Flash-light Project, a national technology assessment initiative sponsored by the Annenburg/CPB and the American Association for Higher Education. By using the items from the Flashlight Project's Current Student Inventory (AAHE, 1997) within the center's own surveys, the university hopes that comparisons of its efforts with those of other universities will ultimately be available.

CONCLUSION

All of Virginia Tech's efforts represent significant resource reallocations (hu-man and financial) to refreshed approaches to instruction, even as they seek to realize the university's productivity aims. These aims are clearly stated in the *University Plan for 1996–2001*. This plan and its companion implementation document, the *Academic Agenda*, identify such goals and strategies as facilitat-ing teaching in a distributed learning environment; facilitating the integration of technology in teaching, research, and outreach; and making creative, effi-cient, and effective use of resources while maintaining and improving student learning.

Having these university goals has set Virginia Tech on a definite path. Yet the newness of the changing instructional landscape at Virginia Tech some-times makes clear description of emergent activities, roles, policies, and pro-grams difficult, especially using traditional terms or organizational structures. What is a purely academic feature of the university or an administrative support function? What is instructional space and who supports its use? Who needs to be involved and what has to happen across an institution and beyond to have various technologies support learning and learners well? Even as advanced communications and information systems have made the world a smaller place, they have also brought the university closer together, in all its rarified parts. Infrastructure, which includes networks, hardware, software, and support for their uses, informs teaching and research applications. Similarly, applications development across the content areas drives the development of infrastructure.

Key leaders at the university believe that it is important, if not critical at this juncture, to keep these two creative avenues—infrastructure and applications development—closely linked. Therefore, since 1996, the chief information officer at Virginia Tech, the vice president for information systems, has re-ported to the president of the university to enable close coordination and oversight. With a budget of over $45 million focused on information systems at Virginia Tech, the new reporting relationship represented a conscious decision to solidify at the highest levels the institution's commitment to integrating technology seamlessly in the fabric of the educational enterprise. As a conse-quence of its progressive efforts, Virginia Tech won the prestigious CAUSE

Award in 1998 for the outstanding manner in which the university has developed, integrated, and supported a sophisticated infrastructure such that it fosters applications development even as it evolves in relation to teaching and learning needs.

Virginia Tech's faculty instructional development story illustrates a successful emergence of structures and roles that must continue to mature if the university is to stay this course. Yet as important as the faculty's ideas and the institution's nascent organizational and recognition efforts are, they will not survive, much less transform teaching and learning over time, without appropriate financial models that support a comprehensive, evolutionary enterprise. Indeed, the next frontier for instructional development and transformation is the creation of adequate, flexible business models that sustain such initiatives. Today some institutions are creating nonprofit and for-profit institutions alongside the existing educational enterprise to allow for more flexibility of operation and foster strategic advantage for themselves in those sectors that are calling for an educational response.

Still other challenges remain. For a public Research I institution like Virginia Tech, such comprehensive aims to integrate technology in instruction and support it appropriately may seem to run counter to the university's continuing need to invent and fund its research agenda. Instead of a view of all boats rising on a new technology-assisted tide, the perspective of a shrinking pie can easily prevail in an enterprise where one and many activities have often subsidized others. At the same time that institutions are attempting to improve teaching, researchers find themselves in a changing sea of research direction and support. As a result, frustration and exhaustion can easily surface in faculty who are bombarded with the labor-intensive activities of reinventing an academic enterprise for a new age, whether in their research or teaching or both.

Moreover, an unrelenting public cry for responsiveness to needs for more flexible approaches to learning over a lifetime and for accountability raises anxiety levels all around. Some of Virginia Tech's 160,000 alumni have already made friendly calls for accounts on both fronts. The good news is that many of these former students look to their alma mater first for reasonably priced responsiveness to their educational needs. Still, the vulnerability of a large, vertically integrated institution to more nimble, network-based information providers has become more salient to faculty and administration alike.

Ironically, the Faculty Development Institute, while attempting to move the institution toward more technology-assisted information processing, also succeeded in putting the university in the vanguard of the much discussed support crisis in information technology. In hindsight it seems clear that the support crisis cannot be fixed by merely adding on more people and programs to assist in a labor-intensive transformation. Although institutionally supported faculty development in instructional technology will help provide skills to those charged with change, substantive shifts in policy, process, and procedure are required for these new approaches to teaching and learning to become established and easily used. Systemic institutional support in the form of rewards and incentives in the promotion process, for example, and even revenue-sharing programs with departments engaged in distance learning and equity-based partnerships for faculty in new learning ventures will be needed for transformation to continue to evolve. These new systemic approaches to supporting technology-assisted programming could be viewed as an investment in learning for the entire enterprise.

Certainly, a primary focus of Virginia Tech's productivity efforts is learning effectiveness. If learning is not improved through these activities, then the university's efforts to reengineer for a modern age will not be worth much.

By spotlighting redesigned learning environments, providing tools to assist reengineering, and creating new models of productive learning environments, Virginia Tech and others are offering substantive content and process worthy of innovative budget and finance arrangements for ongoing instructional development in a modern economy. There are many good reasons for such timely approaches to the next frontier. Yet perhaps the best one is this: based on Virginia Tech's findings to date, many in the university believe that the use of instructional technology when coupled with appropriate instructional design (i.e., course transformation) can indeed improve student learning. By mastering technologies and their best uses in a content area, students can gain the technological competence in content areas that employers demand. Perhaps as important, by actively participating as apprentices in these advanced learning communities, students can also make gains in the self-direction, self-discipline, teamwork, problem solving, communication, and analytical skills for which many sectors of society are calling. These traits will also drive discovery within the university and without.

REFERENCES

Chickering, Arthur W., and Gamson, Zelda (March 1987). "Seven Principles For Good Practice in Undergraduate Education." *AAHE Bulletin.* Washington, DC: American Association For Higher Education.

Information about Virginia Tech's efforts to integrate technology into teaching and learning can be found on the World Wide Web at the following URLs:

Instructional Development Initiative
   http://www.edtech.vt.edu/idi
Center for Innovation in Learning
   http://www.edtech.vt.edu/cil
Cyberschool
   http://www.cyber.vt.edu

ACCESS Project
  http://edtech.vt.edu/access
The Institute for Distance and Distributed Learning
  http://www.dl.vt.edu
The Math Emporium
  http://www.emporium.vt.edu
Net.Work.Virginia
  http://www.networkvirginia.net
Information Systems (with links to other infrastructure initiatives)
  http://www.vt.edu/IS/dir/locovp.html

VIRGINIA TECH'S FACULTY DEVELOPMENT INITIATIVES

Instructional Development Initiative—designed to outfit presentation classrooms for technology-assisted instruction; to establish origination sites for
  distance learning; to create and support the Faculty Development Institute.
  http://www.edtech.vt.edu/idi

Faculty Development Institute—a four-year recurring development program
  that allows all Virginia Tech faculty to learn how to integrate technology
  into instruction; faculty receive equipment and software for participating.
  http://www.edtech.vt.edu

Center for Excellence in Undergraduate Teaching—is charged with enhancing the culture for teaching throughout the university and providing
  direct assistance to faculty in their teaching responsibilities; often plays a
  role in offering grants for technology-assisted instruction.

Cyberschool—a grassroots group of approximately 60 early adopters of using
  technology in teaching; functions as a support network and advocate for
  new policies and initiatives. http://www.cyber.vt.edu

Center for Innovation in Learning—strategically focused, major awards
  program for course development; grants encourage faculty to develop courses,
  programs, and modules in targeted curricular areas. http://www.edtech.vt.edu/
  cil

Center for Distance and Distributed Learning—coordinates the university's
  distance and distributed learning efforts, providing a holistic approach to
  distance learning and identifying niche markets for the university. http://
  www.dl.vt.edu

CHAPTER 6

Developing Faculty Use of Technology

The Bellevue Community College Experience

Kae R. Hutchison

Bellevue Community College (BCC) is a comprehensive, two-year public college serving a group of urban/suburban communities located in the eastern part of the greater Seattle metropolis, an area locally referred to as "the Eastside." With a population exceeding 373,000, the Eastside is a major employment center. Home to Microsoft, a burgeoning number of other software companies, along with medical, biotech, telecommunication, and aircraft electronics companies, the Eastside is experiencing increasing demands for a technologically proficient workforce. BCC serves almost 20,000 students per term, about half of those in credit and half in noncredit offerings. There are approximately 150 full-time faculty and 275 adjunct faculty in credit programs, and another 7 full-time faculty and 380 adjunct faculty in noncredit programs.

BCC is acknowledged in Washington State as a leader in using electronic technology in instruction. It was one of the first community colleges in the region to offer telecourses, using television and/or videos as the primary delivery mechanism, and to develop online courses delivered totally over the Internet. In fall quarter 2000, the college offered 91 fully online courses, 64 of them credit courses and 27 continuing education courses, more than any other college in the state.

To some degree, the college has absorbed and adopted electronic technology by virtue of its location. BCC is fortunate to be centrally located in a technologically sophisticated region, with Boeing a few miles to the south, Microsoft a few miles to the north, and a thriving high-tech business and industrial community all around. Many of BCC's students come with considerable technological sophistication and expectations to match.

The college's high-tech neighborhood has its drawbacks as well: it is increasingly difficult to attract and keep talented faculty and staff when there are so many higher-paid jobs available in the area. BCC has stepped up to the challenge of meeting its community's expectations on a state-agency budget, providing quality learning opportunities to students with a broad range of experience and resources. This chapter describes the structures and culture that have allowed BCC to come to its leadership position

CURRENT PRACTICES: USING TECHNOLOGY IN TEACHING AND LEARNING AT BCC

Change is our middle name. Sometimes it's our first name.

BCC administrator

BCC makes use of instructional technology in many different ways. Instructors employ a variety of electronic instructional tools, including e-mail, electronic slide presentations, Web-based information sources for students, faculty-built Web sites, threaded discussions, and chat rooms. Nearly all faculty use e-mail and most are either active users of some electronic technology in their classrooms or are interested in becoming users.

In the early 1990's, BCC decided it wanted to become a leader in teaching information technology (IT) subjects and providing IT skills to all of its students. Situated in a community that was providing significant worldwide leadership in information technology, the college believed it needed to be aggressive in its efforts to provide the skills needed in the area's workforce. BCC's administrative leadership also believed that the college could not be a leader in teaching IT if the use of technology was confined to a few specialist instructors. Instead the entire college staff and faculty needed to become at least as proficient as BCC wanted its students to be.

The first step in achieving this kind of expertise was to place computers on the desk of every faculty member that wanted one, as well as to provide access to computers for all staff. This move was accomplished in the 1995–1996 academic year. At that time the computers were also networked so that the college community could begin to communicate electronically. Training was made available on a regular basis and college processes began to reward the innovators who stepped forward to learn and use technology. A second important step in widening faculty access to technology was achieved when the college began equipping classrooms with electronic podiums that allowed connection to the Internet and projection devices that provided easy use of other tools such as electronic slide presentations and videos. At about the same time the college leveraged its experience with telecourses to begin supporting faculty who were willing to develop online courses. This infrastructure made it possible to stimulate faculty use of technology so that it expanded to where it is today.

Despite some faculty concerns about the college's emphasis on technology, there is a considerable level of exploration and experimentation with technology and a strong focus on using it to improve student learning. The college administration supports both questioning the educational roles and effectiveness of technology and experimenting with new technologies for student learning. This section examines the many teaching and learning activities at BCC that incorporate instructional technologies introduced on college campuses in the last decade.

Faculty Access to Technology

The technology available for faculty to work with students includes computerized classrooms with stations provided for student work and projection units for the instructors. There are 30 of these classrooms, 19 of them available for credit programs and 11 off-campus rooms managed by Continuing Education. Faculty also have access to 19 electronic classrooms with "smart podium" equipment including a networked computer, VCR unit, and ceiling-mounted projector, and six other classrooms without the network capabilities (both types represent about 18% of all classrooms). Media Services also maintains several mobile computer carts that instructors can schedule for specific days and times. The college will add five more electronic classrooms and will continue its efforts to make the access to technology easier for both faculty and students.

All full-time faculty are provided computers in their offices. Adjunct instructors have access to computers through groups of computers that are placed in each division office area. All faculty and staff receive support for their office computers from a centralized help center that includes professional staff and student interns who can respond immediately to software issues, and from technical staff who can assist with hardware and more complex software problems. The Help Desk is available 8 A.M. to 5 P.M. during the workweek. Currently the college is planning on a four-year replacement schedule for its 700 faculty and staff computers, with priority for updates given to the faculty who are teaching technology and need higher-end or more recent systems to do so or who are the most intense users, and to those whose computers are below the college's current minimum standards. A centralized budget has been created (averaging approximately $125,000 or an average of $175 per employee computer station) to underwrite half the cost of each year's upgrades, with the employee's unit providing the other half.

Instructional Uses of Technology

Instructors use electronic technology in a variety of ways at BCC. Although online courses are often featured when the college talks about its use of technology, other classroom-based uses are predominant. In a community where over two-thirds of our students tell us they have access to the Internet, many instructors are combining e-mail communication and classroom instruction. Instructors use Web sites to provide basic information about their courses and refer students to resources. Other instructors create simulations or gather resources such as photographs or art examples and make them available on their Web site or bring them into the classroom to illustrate concepts. Our library staff has provided active leadership in teaching classroom instructors how to incorporate the Web into their assignments and showing students how to perform good electronic research.

Periodically the college creates opportunities to share what faculty members are doing so that the experiments and learning of those who have moved ahead can inform and spark interest in others. Faculty hold seminars on particular projects, are featured at professional development days, share their projects at division unit meetings, and are showcased in college publications. Workshops are scheduled quarterly to provide faculty an overview of what is involved in creating online courses and training is offered for all faculty who are creating online courses. The Faculty Resource Center holds "brown bag" lunch meetings for faculty to discuss issues related to their online courses.

The following sections provide more detail on a number of the areas in which faculty are using technology in their teaching.

Distance Education and Distributed Learning

Distance education has a long history at BCC, beginning in 1977 when the college offered the nationally developed "Roots" course over its cable channel. The very positive response to this course stimulated the college's interest in developing additional distance courses for students, even though the college is a single campus with a relatively compact service area of 817 square miles (about 25% of that area is mountains). The college purchased courses from outside vendors (after screening by BCC faculty) and supported BCC faculty in developing their own courses. Only a few faculty members were interested in creating telecourses and initially there was serious debate as to whether telecourses provided the same quality of instruction as the in-class mode. Enrollment in BCC's telecourses started slowly and expanded gradually until the mid-1990s, peaking 1997–1998. Telecourse enrollment appears to be gradually declining as online courses become more prevalent. Total telecourse enrollment was 1,441 in 1996–1997, 1,755 in 1997–1998, 1,644 in 1998–1999, and 1,409 in 1999–2000.

Online courses offered via the Internet followed a similar pattern of a rather slow start coupled with concern over quality and equivalency. The acceptance and expansion phases have come very quickly, however, and enrollments are on a rapid upward trajectory: 61 students in 1996–1997, 437 in 1997–1998, 1,573 in 1998–1999, 3,706 in 1999–2000. Based on summer, fall and winter actual figures, over 6300 enrollments are projected for 2000/2001. In 1999-2000 BCC offered over 60 different credit online courses and scheduled a total of 157 credit online sections. In contrast to telecourses, BCC faculty (both full and adjunct) have developed all credit online courses locally. All courses have also been "online" versions of already existing courses rather than totally new curricula. A Distance Learning Committee meets regularly to review tele-course and online course offerings, to make recommendations on general direction and faculty training needs, and to advise on contract issues being negotiated between the college administration and the faculty bargaining unit.

Hybrid courses, called "distributed learning," are proving to be an exciting use of instructional technology. Distributed learning combines elements of the new instructional technology with elements of the face-to-face classroom, such as posting materials on the Web and using e-mail to communicate. BCC's online instructors have been leaders in incorporating instructional techniques from their online courses into their face-to-face classrooms; other instructors are discovering they also like the options these technologies offer for students.

Computer-assisted Learning Labs

BCC's reading, writing, and math labs (which all began in the 1970s as tutorial centers) provide a combination of computer-assisted learning and one-on-one help for students, usually from peer tutors. The learning labs are directed by full-time faculty who also carry regular teaching assignments, a combination that helps to keep the labs synchronized with departmental curricula and teaching and learning objectives. Learning labs have been organized at BCC over time as departments and divisions identified students' needs and sought ways to provide additional learning time outside the classroom. This process continues: an ESL learning lab was established five years ago and a science learning lab opened in fall 2000.

Student Access to Technology

Because basic computer literacy has become a requirement for higher educa-tion, student access to technology has become a major concern for the college. Even though more and more students have computers and Internet accounts at home or elsewhere, BCC acknowledges the responsibility to provide sufficient access on campus. The college provides an e-mail account and generous computer time for all students so that faculty can legitimately require the use of e-mail and online resources. An open computer lab in the college's technology building is fully networked and available about 90 hours per week. Another 12 Internet terminals are available for student use in the Library-Media Center. Students also have access to the computer-assisted learning labs previously described for work in reading, writing, and math. In all there are over 1,200 computers available to students, approximately one for every eight students enrolled in credit programs.

In 1997, students voted to implement a universal technology access fee of $1.80 per credit (maximum of $18) in order to support wide access to computers. In 1999, they increased the fee to $3.50 per credit (up to a maximum of $35) to ensure a three-year replacement cycle for the computers used by students. These universal student technology fees provide major financial support for the student labs. Additional computer-use fees are attached to certain BCC classes with significant computer lab time requirements. The proliferation of fees is a concern to many in the campus community, but the additional funding is critical to maintaining appropriate hardware, software, and e-mail service and to providing lab supervisors and other assistance to keep student access to technology open and functioning smoothly.

Students may bring in their own computers and access the college Internet and online services in a few classrooms. The college is not yet able to provide students this kind of access in the library or in informal areas such as the student lounges, although the buildings have been designed to accommodate that in the future, and the college plans to install that capacity in the next two years.

ORGANIZATIONAL STRUCTURES THAT SUPPORT FACULTY DEVELOPMENT

> Whatever we are doing, it is keeping our faculty productive, charged up, and innovative.
>
> President Jean Floten

BCC encourages faculty development and supports instructors' learning in a number of ways. These include an annual allocation for professional development and two "professional development days" set aside in the college calendar each year for activities planned by a faculty Professional Development Committee. The annual professional development allocation flows to instructional divisions at the rate of $1,150 per full-time faculty position (the college has 150 full-time faculty and 275 adjunct faculty teaching in credit programs), and is intended to provide support primarily for full-time but also for adjunct faculty.

The college's self-support continuing education program and international intensive English programs do not participate in this professional development pool. Each division determines how its allocation is spent, with input from the division faculty. A faculty committee organizes activities for the two professional development days and is supported by the Executive Dean of Instruction's office with annual expenditures of about $5,000. Activities at two additional "college issues days" are planned by the administration. Summer grants are awarded to faculty projects, with priorities for funding guided by current college initiatives. Individual grants are usually from $500 to $1,500, and the college dedicates from $35,000 to $50,000 (including benefits) to these activities.

Most of these mechanisms for faculty development have existed at the college for several decades. One of the newer avenues for faculty development is the Faculty Resource Center that was established in 1995. At first focused on assisting faculty in the use of technology, it is now staffed to provide help with curriculum design *and* technology. In addition, BCC's successful self-support distance education program pays faculty members to develop new online courses and telecourses. Faculty interested in developing a distance course apply to the Associate Dean of Information Technology. The Associate Dean works collaboratively with the division chairs to ensure that the distance courses and faculty selected have their support. He gives priority to courses that will help complete or expand BCC's distance degree and certificate options. Once approved, a faculty member receives two-thirds released time for one quarter (or an equivalent stipend) to develop the course. After the course is developed and offered, the faculty developer receives $10 per enrolled student (regardless of who is teaching the course) to keep the distance course materials up to date.

Most of BCC's means of supporting faculty development can be found at other colleges and universities. What is perhaps unique to BCC is the total level of funding provided through all the sources (approximately 1.6% of the budget), and the strong institutional commitment to growth and improvement for all instructors. The most significant areas of support for technology are described more fully.

Training Available to all BCC Employees

BCC provides faculty and staff a variety of ongoing training opportunities, primarily concerned with the use of administrative and instructional technology. The Faculty Resource Center coordinates staff training workshops throughout the year, covering standard topics such as e-mail, electronic scheduling, word processing, spreadsheets, and databases as well as more advanced workshops such as Web site design and use of the Internet. The NorthWest Center for Emerging Technology (NWCET), a National Science Foundation (NSF) project that is housed in BCC's technology building, also offers technology training targeted to educators in the state and its offerings are readily available to faculty on the campus.

Faculty and staff are encouraged to register for Continuing Education classes and workshops on a space-available basis at a discounted price (often paid for by the division or department). These classes may be taken during work hours or on evenings and weekends, as schedules permit. Special presentations and training sessions have frequently been incorporated into Opening Week activities before the academic year starts, or on the college's two non-instructional Professional Development Days. For the past several years, Help Desk student interns have been available on Professional Development Days to come to any faculty or staff office for one-on-one tutorials.

Faculty Professional Development Funding

One of the strongest forms of support is the faculty professional development allocation. For nearly a decade, BCC has provided a generous annual allocation per full-time faculty member for professional development (currently $1,150). These funds are pooled in the division and distributed to full-time and adjunct faculty to support specific learning goals. Faculty members often use these funds to keep up to date in their discipline, attending conferences and other traditional professional development activities. Many BCC faculty are active members of national discipline associations. There are also statewide Conferences on assessment, interdisciplinary studies, and diversity that faculty may choose to attend. Faculty may use the professional development funds to pay tuition for credit or noncredit courses that expand their expertise, including specialized technology applications from our extensive Continuing Education offerings.

When computers first came onto the campus, many faculty used the professional development funds to buy desktop computers for their offices. In more recent years, the college has provided the basic funding for faculty computers and software. Some faculty still choose to use professional development money to upgrade or purchase specialized applications.

Summer Grants Program

Another significant avenue for curriculum and technology development is the BCC Summer Grant program administered by the Instruction office and funded from a variety of sources, including National Science Foundation grants, federal and state vocational training funds, and the President's and Dean's discretionary budgets. Instructors (both full-time and adjunct) may apply for funding to work on special projects, working individually or in teams. The administration determines which types of projects will be given high priority, using these priorities to provide impetus for key college initiatives. For the last seven years, technology-related projects have received high priority and faculty have responded with a substantial number of projects ranging from producing new interdisciplinary courses to designing and implementing complex Web sites. A total of $35,000–$50,000 (including benefits) is spent annually on these projects. Awards range from the cost of one or two Continuing Education computer classes to several thousand dollars.

Faculty Resource Center

The Faculty Resource Center (FRC) was conceived in the early 1990s when the college was planning for a technology center. Start-up funding for the FRC provided a position to assist faculty with technology, and came from a major NSF grant received by BCC in 1995 to develop curriculum standards for information technology careers. The NorthWest Center for Emerging Technology (NWCET) is the organization that now guides the NSF work. In 1998, the NWCET and the FRC moved into a new technology building that provided a permanent home for this faculty support function. The NWCET continues to support one FRC position and the college now supports two positions (an information technology specialist and a curriculum design specialist).

Each quarter three to five student interns from the Media Communications & Technology department are available to help instructors prepare materials (scanning, digital photography, image enhancement, etc.) and develop Web pages. Collectively, these students work on 8 to 15 faculty or staff projects each quarter. The FRC was instrumental in making the decision to pick a standard package (WebCT) for Web-based course development and management. FRC staff offers regular workshops about using it to create and implement online courses. They have also developed a Web-based tutorial for placing materials on the Internet.

Student Intern Assistance

One of BCC's most successful approaches is to involve students directly in bringing technology into teaching and learning. BCC students in our technology programs provide a tremendous resource as they teach the teachers in other programs and provide campus support. For example, students in the Media programs regularly design Web pages for departments or individual faculty members, and student interns at the Faculty Resource Center help translate course materials into online format. Information Technology/Technical Support students also provide "tutorials" on faculty/staff professional development days.

Distance Education Development Contracts

BCC's Distance Education contract for development of credit telecourses and online courses is another mechanism that encourages BCC faculty involvement with technology. It also maintains certain institutional standards and safeguards. An instructor planning to develop a telecourse or online course can enter into a formal agreement with the Distance Education Program, which then provides two-thirds released time for one quarter (or an equivalent stipend). The contract requires a course outline and development timeline plus signatures from the department and division chairs. It includes stipulations that ensure the content will be equal to traditional course offerings and is sufficiently generic that other instructors can use it. It makes it clear that ownership of the materials resides with the college; however, the college also commits to negotiating with the faculty member prior to selling or leasing any course. This agreement applies only to distance education contracts and is not in place for other curricular materials developed by faculty. The contract also provides the faculty member a continuing $10 fee per student to support the cost of ongoing course updates. To date the college has lease agreements for three of its courses, all being used for "tech-prep" support by a K–12 district.

In Continuing Education, development of online courses has been supported by providing training to interested faculty and paying a $600 stipend to faculty who want to develop an online course. Faculty who develop online courses for continuing education get a 50/50 split of the course income each time the course is offered—an arrangement that is not standard for most continuing education courses. More recently, Continuing Education has purchased the core online curriculum from outside vendors and asked a faculty member to develop a local focus for the materials and exercises and conduct the course online. In some instances, faculty come to BCC with preexisting courses they have designed and we add them to our offerings.

Intellectual Property Agreements

In some instances, faculty members choose to develop curriculum materials, including new Web-based resources, with their own equipment and on their own time. For these cases the college has drafted a standard agreement acknowledging the instructor's ownership of intellectual property rights in those materials so that there can be little confusion about violations of the state's ethics law or royalties from sale of the materials.

In Continuing Education, there is no arrangement at present that clarifies ownership of course materials developed by faculty who have been paid a stipend. The program has not yet had to face what happens if those faculty choose to leave the college.

Intangible Incentives for Faculty Participation

Many of the incentives Bellevue Community College offers faculty are quite concrete, such as the faculty professional development funds and the Summer Grant program. Although harder to describe, intangible incentives are just as important in getting faculty to use new technologies. At BCC, the most significant of the "intangibles" is an institutional culture that values new ideas and embraces change. The college's faculty and staff have a long tradition of finding ways to get new things done, despite organizational hurdles and limited resources. This tradition and culture permeate the institution from the ground up as well as from the top down.

Keeping BCC at the forefront of technology in education was a stated Board initiative from 1992 through 1995 and has since become one of the "givens" of the institution. BCC very consciously strives to stay on the leading edge in both instructional and administrative uses of technology at all levels, and President B. Jean Floten (1989 to the present) has been a significant force in maintaining that consciousness. One of the core missions of the college as defined in 1994 is to be "a leader and partner in the culture, technology, and business of our Eastside community." An institutional culture that genuinely values innovation supports experimentation with new instructional technologies. The college provides a nurturing environment for the instructor taking the first hesitant steps toward using e-mail as well as for the instructor launching a major new program—and possibly a career change—within the institution. The general institutional culture and environment contribute immeasurably to helping faculty learn to use technology.

Strategic Planning for Technology

Bellevue Community College has put together strategic plans for the acquisition and use of information technology at several points in the last decade. Impetus for some of the planning comes from outside the college. The community college's system technology organization, the Center for Information Services, provides support for the administrative computing systems at all community and technical colleges in the state and requires periodic updates to campus technology plans. BCC's own internal planning processes are more significant in guiding college activities.

With strong guidance from President Floten, a team of administrators and faculty members worked on a strategic plan for the college in 1990–1992. This planning process identified creation of a technology center as a high priority for the college. This plan became the launch for a major fund-raising campaign throughout BCC's community. It also set the stage for the college's grant proposal to the National Science Foundation to become a center for Advanced Technology Education, the grant that established the NWCET. The plans were adjusted when the college secured the NSF grant award and an opportunity to co-locate the State Archives on the BCC campus arose. A new plan was created in 1996, and has guided the college for the past four years. With most of the 1996 goals achieved, the college completed a new technology plan in fall 2000.

Another, more recent planning breakthrough is the establishment of a computer equipment capitalization fund and process. For the first two years of this process, the college has allocated an annual average of $125,000 to a centralized budget, to be used for systematically upgrading and/or replacing faculty and staff desktop systems. The need for a capitalization plan has been under discussion for nearly a decade; the funds were finally allocated during the 1998–1999 planning and budgeting process.

Administrative Positions and Organization

Over the past decade, Bellevue Community College has made a number of organizational changes to reflect new circumstances. A new administrative position, Dean of Information Resources, was created in 1993. Until that time, administrative systems had been the responsibility of the Dean (later Vice President) of Administrative Services while responsibility for instructional computing was dispersed throughout Instruction. Instruction's decentralized structure had evolved over time as new technologies were embraced and programs created in different divisions or areas of the college organization. During a campus-wide reorganization effort in 1994–1995, consensus was reached that the decentralized structure was no longer serving the college well. The first change moved all student labs under the Dean of Information Resources. A second change moved Distance Education and the Media Communications & Technology department into a new, independent Telecommunications division in 1997–1998.

In 1998, a reorganization in the Instruction Office created a dean's position that was assigned a focus on professional development. Restructuring in January 2001 will move that professional development assignment to a faculty member with released time, and will include responsibility for working with the Faculty Professional Development Committee as well as the Summer Grant and new faculty orientation processes. This position will participate in the Educational Services Cabinet, a group that combines all instructional units with representatives from Student Services and Information Resources. Through these connections, this position helps ensure that strategic college priorities are reflected in the college's varied professional development processes.

An additional restructuring that was begun in summer 2000 was the movement of all workforce development and continuing education to report to a new Vice President of Workforce Development. This structure is designed to allow the college to provide a quick and coordinated response to the growing demands for workforce training. After being filled for seven months with an interim vice president, the structure will be completed in 2001 after the new permanent vice president joins the college in February.

BCC's fall 2000 organizational structure is illustrated in Figure 6.1.

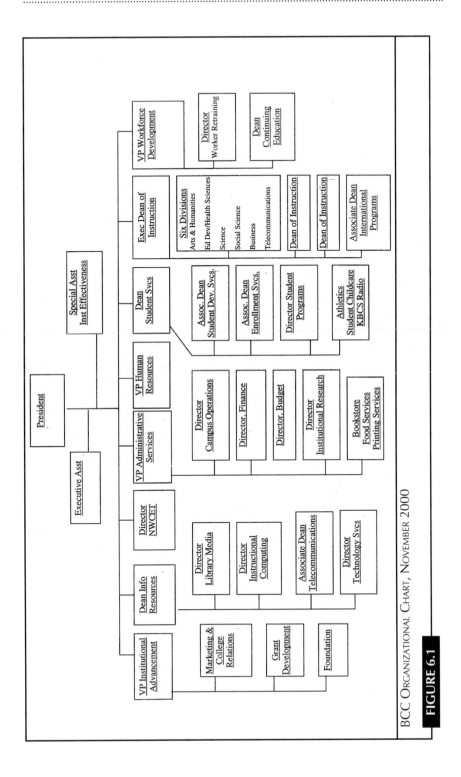

BCC ORGANIZATIONAL CHART, NOVEMBER 2000

FIGURE 6.1

Centralization and Standardization

One of the hazards of BCC's bottom-up approach to innovation is that it can lead to an unmanageable proliferation of different hardware and software in departments with different functions, priorities, and resources. Some inequities among the instructional divisions arose because of this approach. Others occurred because when computers were first introduced, some departments had self-supporting programs or other funding mechanisms that could pay for equipment, while others did not. As the use of technology expanded, the strain on the college's support capabilities and resources became more and more pronounced. In the early 1990s, it became clear that one backbone was required to strengthen both administrative and instructional uses of technology. When the administration committed itself to providing networked computers throughout the college, it made the decision to limit hardware and software options to achieve a supportable system. The college now supports one PC platform and a Macintosh platform, along with a limited range of software.

Planning and Budgeting Process

Another organizational structure that supports faculty development is BCC's comprehensive planning and budgeting process, first developed in 1995–1996 and still being refined. The process encourages ideas for innovation at the departmental level. Proposals submitted by departments are reviewed and prioritized within divisions, then within major areas (instruction, student services, administrative services, etc.), then at the college-wide level. The President's Staff ranks all proposals to receive funding as it becomes available during budget development. Frequently President's Staff can help identify self-support or other outside funding sources to support the plans. Each proposal must be clearly linked to the college's goals and the Board of Trustees' initiatives. This system encourages new ideas from the bottom up while ensuring overall direction and coordination. Planning and budgeting proposals can include requests for equipment, new staff positions, released time for development and training, and so on.

Institutional Efforts to Secure Alternative Funding

State allocations frequently do not cover all continuing operating expenses, much less the equipment, time, and training required to incorporate advanced technology into college programs and services. BCC's focus on technology-based professional development and innovation in instruction has required vigorous pursuit of alternative funding sources, including

- BCC Foundation fund raising, which provided the first multimedia lab on campus and later brought in community support for the NWCET building.

- Self-support instructional programs outside the state full-time equivalent student allocations, such as Distance Education, International Students, and Continuing Education.
- Profitable operation of BCC enterprises such as the bookstore and cafeteria.
- Partnerships with local high-tech businesses and industries.
- Grant sources such as the National Science Foundation, U.S. Department of Labor, state technology initiative funds, state worker retraining funds, and so on.

As a whole, the college has for many years encouraged pursuit of these alternatives as a supplement to its state funds. For 2000–2001, excluding tuition, state general fund allocations represent just 39% of BCC's annual budget of $52.3 million, a marked change from a decade ago when it represented about twice that percentage.

MAJOR FACULTY TECHNOLOGY DEVELOPMENT INITIATIVES

In addition to ongoing mechanisms supporting faculty development, there have been several initiatives that have focused specifically on developing BCC's instructional technology capacities. The Board of Trustees selected technology as one of its strategic initiatives for the college in 1992; for the next three years, technology training was a strong component of faculty professional development days and additional workshops to assist faculty in learning to use technology were offered throughout the academic year. Summer Grants also focused heavily on technology skills development. Two other college initiatives focused on technology are now described.

Critical Thinking and Information Literacy Across the Curriculum (CTILAC)

The "Critical Thinking and Information Literacy Across the Curriculum" project (CTILAC, pronounced "Catillac") was piloted in 1996 with five faculty members. Impetus for the project came from the Library-Media Center, which defines "information literacy" to include basic library skills, text-and Internet-based research techniques, and problem-solving strategies. This project grew out of concerns by library staff about the abilities of both faculty and students to access and wisely use Internet-based materials. Expanded and funded by the National Science Foundation in 1998, CTILAC has a range of objectives for faculty and students, including:

- Improved faculty skills in locating information using electronic resources.

- Curriculum revisions with greater emphasis on critical thinking and information literacy skills.
- Classroom assignments incorporating discipline-specific critical thinking and information literacy skills and resources.
- Increased technology skills and applications.

For the past four years, a group of faculty from different disciplines was selected each year to participate in the project. The project provides the equivalent of 17 sections of released time to give faculty members the opportunity to participate and contribute. Participating faculty mentored other BCC faculty, as well as presented workshops regionally and nationally. Although NSF funding stopped in January 2001, the college expects the work and expertise generated by the project to continue its impact on BCC curriculum. Some of the materials produced by faculty for CTILAC are available at http://ir.bcc.ctc.edu/library/ilac/default.htm.

NorthWest Center for Emerging Technologies

The NorthWest Center for Emerging Technologies (NWCET) was established on the BCC campus in 1995 with support from a six-year, $5 million National Science Foundation grant. The NWCET's overarching goal is to advance education in information technology to meet the region's need for an IT-skilled workforce. The NWCET motto is "preparing knowledge workers of the future" and the focus is on fostering partnerships linking business, education, and government; developing curriculum products and services, including online course material; and creating pathways to IT and advanced technology degree programs. The NWCET sponsors workshops and conferences and its showcase publication, *Building a Foundation for Tomorrow: Skill Standards for Information Technology*, is widely used in IT training programs around the country.

Faculty Resource Center staff and other BCC faculty are closely involved in developing and testing NWCET courseware and curriculum modules. While many of the curriculum titles center around teaching information technology itself (database administration, programming, technical support, media communication & technology, computer networking), the NWCET also looks at IT in relationship to other disciplines. Recent titles include English composition for IT, technical report writing for IT, science skills for IT, and math and science for media technology. NWCET work is delineating how other fields contribute to instruction in information technology at the same time that other departments at BCC are exploring how information technology contributes to instruction in their various disciplines.

IMPACTS ON TEACHING AND LEARNING

It has changed the way I teach.

BCC faculty member

In a word, the chief impact of technology on both teaching and learning at BCC is "options." Students have more options for accessing the college and more options for fitting courses into their complex personal schedules. Faculty have more options for organizing the learning experiences of students and for interacting with students. Some instructors also are beginning to use technology to restructure the way they spend their work time with the college.

Many of the impacts on both teaching and learning are still anecdotal rather than formally assessed. In the early days of using telecourses, BCC did a study that compared the grades of students who were taking parallel sections of the same course taught as a telecourse and as a classroom-based course, often taught by the same instructor. The college did not find significant differences in students' achievements on tests. The college repeated a similar study when it began developing online courses, with similar results. It is evident that students are capable of learning the material at a similar level in both modes. BCC has found higher noncompletion rates in its distance courses than its average for classroom courses. We do not know whether this is due to a lack of faculty expertise when first using this new mode, the difficulties some students have in adjusting to a new mode of learning, or to problems with the technology itself. The college has responded by developing better processes and self-use materials to help distance students, especially online students, understand the self-organizational and technological skills they will need to be successful, and by increasing the level of technical support it provides to online students. It also continues its work with instructors to increase their skills with the technology.

Early in our development of both telecourses and online courses it became evident that teaching with these technologies required the instructor to re-think the course structure and content. These media do not work well unless the entire course is fairly carefully laid out and scripted, and unless faculty are clear about what they want students to be able to do at the end of the course. While there is still flexibility to adjust as the course unfolds, there is less room to improvise large segments of the course or to wait well into the quarter before organizing the materials for the latter part of the course. Online course development has created as much impetus for faculty to carefully identify student outcomes as have the initiatives that have been directly focused on outcomes and assessment.

The online environment provides a number of benefits to student learning. Access to materials online enables students to review as frequently as necessary to master the concepts, assisting students who learn at different paces. Links to related material mean that curious and motivated students can explore other avenues. Sophisticated simulations and illustrations of concepts can be developed using multimedia technology that are simply not possible with traditional teaching tools. E-mail allows individual communication with the instructor and BCC instructors report that they have more interactions with students in this online environment that they normally do in the classroom. Chat rooms and threaded discussions augment in-class discussion and provide opportunities for students to express themselves in different ways. Another benefit is that the discussions are preserved, so a student can refer back to them and a faculty member can excerpt and display particular "good passages" illustrating certain key points.

Instructors in classroom courses are now using much of this same electronic technology. The attractions of the online mode are evidenced by the rapid growth of the distributed learning model. Classes that met in the classroom for lecture and discussion five days a week in the past may now meet on campus two or three days, with the remainder of the time online. This combination allows use of the best features of each mode. For example, knowing that the resources will be available online frees students to listen and participate more fully in class without feeling pressured to capture every word in their notes. "Virtual office hours" when students can expect responses to e-mails can supplement on-campus time.

Many faculty working in online and distributed instruction feel that a combination of instructional media is more effective than any single medium. In a distributed course, the online elements reinforce the learning and the in-class sessions provide personal contact and continuity. "Face-to-face" time is still essential for students who are uncomfortable or inexperienced with the technology-based components—and for students who may not have the discipline to pursue their learning entirely independently. Even though the college has not yet created a mechanism to identify and track distributed courses, it knows there are over a hundred courses that regularly combine in-class and online elements. Student reaction has been overwhelmingly positive. Some BCC leaders think that the spin-off into distributed courses is a major benefit of the college's efforts to encourage wholly online distance education.

CONCLUSIONS: LESSONS LEARNED, NEXT STEPS

> I call it infection theory. You infect one faculty member and they talk to others and show them what they are doing with technology. And so the disease spreads.
>
> BCC administrator

BCC's tradition of bottom-up rather than top-down initiatives has both strengths and drawbacks. Faculty incentives such as professional development funds and summer grants are directed by individual instructors' interests and needs rather than by college-wide goals. BCC has relied on the self-starters to provide the early impetus for change and provides many "safe" opportunities for others to take incremental steps in the use of instructional technology. This approach can result in lags and gaps. It can take some time for an innovation to move from the pathfinders into the mainstream of teaching and learning. One important lesson learned is to not rush the development process. BCC's patience is being rewarded. The college appears to have crossed a critical threshold, where most of our faculty are now interested in using technology to facilitate their instruction.

Change takes time; change also often takes money. Most colleges have already learned that there will never be enough money in the operating budgets to support technology needs or desires. BCC has accepted this and moved on to identifying and tapping into nontraditional funding sources. BCC's pattern has been to buy as much technology as the college can afford at the moment, then search for support for the follow-on costs. This pattern is not ideal, and providing sufficient support staff for technology tends to lag behind equipment. BCC's curriculum and planning/budgeting processes are currently being revised to better capture the maintenance and staffing implications of new requests for technology equipment.

If Bellevue Community College were to offer advice to other colleges concerned about teaching faculty to use new technology, it might include:

- Don't worry too much about false starts and dead ends. They're part of the learning process.
- Acknowledge the built-in tensions between individual and institutional perspectives. Pathfinders and pioneers are valuable; centralization and standardization are also valuable.
- Remember that instructional technology is a tool, not a cure-all.
- Recognize that one size *doesn't* fit all. For some instructors, learning to use e-mail or a standard word-processing program to type up quiz and exam questions is a major technological breakthrough.
- Provide a variety of ongoing training opportunities; provide time to take and absorb the training; allow repeat training as often as necessary. Put material online for faculty use after the training.
- Give faculty time—time to learn about new technologies, time to learn to use the tools, time to incorporate the new approaches incrementally, time to fully exploit the possibilities, time to create a new baseline for future innovation.

- Use faculty members as evangelists to other faculty members.
- Showcase faculty work with your other faculty and with off-campus groups.
- Provide a central location for faculty to get help.
- Listen to the voices on campus that object to the amount of attention and resources technology is getting. Nurture the whole teaching and learning environment to encourage new ideas in all arenas. For example, to counter comments from arts and humanities faculty members that all money is going to technology, BCC's president challenged the liberal arts faculty to develop innovative ideas and the president set aside funds to support competitive proposals.
- Keep students at the center of the endeavor. Remember why you are using technology.
- Allocate sufficient funding to ensure that faculty have the technology tools and training to match their interest.

Future Directions

Anticipating where technology will take teaching and learning, or even the higher education enterprise, is like trying to anticipate what is just over the hill as you are driving. You have a rough sense of the terrain, and you can see a certain distance ahead, but the unseen landscape reveals itself just a little at a time, with occasional glimpses of larger spans of territory. From where BCC is currently driving on the road, here are a few of the things we see.

We expect our online courses to continue their dramatic expansion rates for the next several years. Our student population is growing, we do not have sufficient facilities to expand to meet the demand, and increasing numbers of students are "time-bound" and asking for asynchronous options for their courses. Our face-to-face classrooms will continue to change their look, as more and more instructors use e-mail and Web-based components in their courses. In the next five years we anticipate that the majority of faculty will use at least some online components in their classroom-based courses.

Increased use of online components will mean changes in the pattern of campus classrooms. Already some courses are meeting fewer times on campus and faculty are conducting one-third to over one-half of the course online. Our weekend courses are finding the combined mode of some classroom, some online, very attractive. Courses may meet several weeks on campus, then several weeks online. These options have interesting implications for facilities scheduling and planning, as well as patterns of automobile traffic. We predict that, left untended, 25% of our courses might move to this mode in the next three years. With formal encouragement, perhaps more will choose to do so.

Our online students are causing us to rethink all of our processes to see what we can provide without having people drive to the campus. We will be moving to "24 x 7" services being available through the Web and development of self-help materials that assist students in answering questions and getting information on their own. At the same time we are rethinking our internal processes and providing mechanisms for faculty to complete paperwork online. We have implemented a new online tool for submitting grades that also allows faculty to check their current student roster, and are building toward better advising information for faculty. We have just created online forms for submission of all curriculum proposal materials. This will allow us to capture that information electronically, give us the potential of placing it on a Web site and provides the opportunity for faculty to easily access their own or others' work that could be useful in designing new courses or revising existing ones.

Increasing use of technology will impact a number of key institutional processes. BCC's faculty and administration are discussing how to redefine faculty workloads to move away from "seat time" to measures that allow for different patterns of physical presence on the campus. We have redefined office hours to include online time with students. We are also exploring what participation in governance might mean in an environment in which many faculty might not be on campus five days a week, or even at the same time. We expect that state funding mechanisms will lag behind our own work in redefining workload and performance measurements, creating tensions as we attempt to respond to this less structured environment.

The college will need to find ways to make our faculty positions attractive for technology-adept professionals who can easily find higher-paying work. This means reexamining pay structures, support for faculty, the tenure process, governance expectations, and the entire work environment. For example, our tenure process is being revised to assure that the workload involved in developing new technology solutions is recognized and rewarded. There are even questions being raised by some of our newer technology faculty about the value of tenure—which they see as a heavy impact and as less valuable or necessary to them. Our hiring processes are being revised to ensure screening for technology skills.

The college will be investing in mechanisms that use the Web to share materials developed by faculty. Given the amount of time it takes to develop these Web materials, many of which have broader potential than the course for which they were developed, the college wants to open up these materials for other faculty use. Innovations in technology will force revisions in courses to match the new options such as streaming video or face-to-face chats. Faculty will move from being worried about establishing relationships in the online environment to developing mechanisms to control the level of interaction and the "24 x 7" expectations of students so that they are manageable. The technology will continue to revolutionize itself, so we will continue to deal with the workload associated with revising online materials to match the increasing expectations of students and faculty.

CHAPTER 7

The California State University Center for Distributed Learning

Charles Schneebeck and Gerard L. Hanley

In the past few years, a growing number of faculty have wanted to use the World Wide Web to increase the options for learning and teaching. They are encouraged by an increasingly robust technical infrastructure in which networked computers are becoming readily available to students both within the campuses and beyond. The technical tools and the World Wide Web have also created an environment in which virtually any member of the higher education community can create and publish learning materials. They are no longer dependent on being selected by a publisher or other commercial entity to get their work in front of a significant number of their colleagues and students. Yet they are faced with a number of barriers that are slowing the incorporation of technology into the world of learning.

Many universities provide funding for faculty to create Web-based learning materials. But more often than not, there is no viable evaluation mechanism to assure quality, nor is there a dissemination strategy. Occasionally, faculty will produce a learning application that is in high demand for learning and teaching. This creates a situation in which the creator must support the "product," effectively shifting the author's role to that of support staff. Such products are extremely difficult to sustain. Also, high-quality Web-based learning materials that do exist on the Web are difficult to find using standard search engines. And few universities are meeting the demand for technology support staff who play a critical role in supporting faculty and student use of the World Wide Web for learning and teaching. These are some of the barriers that the

California State University Center for Distributed Learning (CDL at www.cdl.edu) was established to address.

In 1993, the California State University (CSU) began a comprehensive planning process, the Integrated Technology Strategy (ITS), to address how technology was being implemented and supported across the CSU system. The process began with an assessment of the current state followed by a visioning exercise for the future state of technology in the system. The focus was not technology; rather it was what the CSU stood for as an institution and what it wanted to stand for in the future.

The ITS took a comprehensive "systems" approach. Planning was based on the premise that effective use of technology requires individual access to a network connection, hardware, software, and training support. These baseline infrastructure components are necessary to realize the four desired outcomes of the ITS planning process: (1) increase personal productivity, (2) support excellence in learning and teaching, (3) assure the quality of student experience, and (4) increase administration productivity and quality (see Figure 7.1).

Clearly, the desired outcomes would not be realized simply by building the baseline infrastructure. Technology initiatives were created to provide a mechanism for stakeholders to focus on critical issues and to create implementation strategies necessary to achieve the desired outcomes. In 1997, the CSU Office

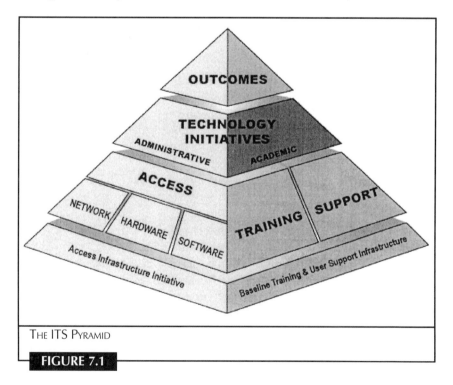

THE ITS PYRAMID

FIGURE 7.1

of the Chancellor opened the CDL to implement the academic technology initiatives: the Distributed Learning and Teaching Initiative and the Multimedia Repository Initiative.

Thus the mission of the CDL is to support those engaged in teaching and learning through the development and dissemination of tools, best practices, and strategies that effectively employ the World Wide Web and related technologies in concert with the CSU's Integrated Technology Strategy.

The CDL does not serve a single campus, but serves the CSU System, which consists of 23 campuses, spread over the state of California. Student enrollment in the system is approximately 340,000, and there is a substantial additional number of students in extended education programs. The system has approximately 18,000 faculty.

The CDL operates with a staff of five full-time employees consisting of a director, program manager, project coordinator, programmer/analyst, distributed learning specialist, and administrative assistant. This small team is able to provide leadership and project management for implementation teams that range from 6 to 160 participants. When possible, team members are recruited from the CSU, but may come from other educational institutions or the private sector. This reality has forced the CDL to address issues of how to facilitate effective group efforts in virtual organizations when the members are geographically dispersed.

These parameters placed the CDL in the role of identifying and managing projects that involve faculty and staff from multiple campuses, a task that does not map neatly to the normal way of doing business. To function effectively, the CDL used planning documents that resulted from system-wide studies.

Activities of the CDL are guided by two documents that were produced in the ITS planning process: Planning Assumptions (http://cdl.edu/html/plassump.html) and Planning Principles (http://cdl.edu/html/plprin.html). Planning Assumptions identify forces that will affect both the planning and implementation of information technology initiatives. These assumptions reflect the current state of the CSU operating environment. Planning Principles set the strategic direction and framework for the use of information technology to achieve the CSU mission and vision for the future. These principles are the source of the criteria used to create, select, design, and implement information technology initiatives and projects.

Perhaps the most useful document for the daily operations of the CDL is the Standards and Criteria for Selecting Projects (http://www.cdl.edu/html/standcr.html). It provides guidelines for choosing the kinds of projects the CDL should do, and the criteria that should be used to select projects. These criteria are critical to the operation of the CDL. They guide the project selection activities and the decisions regarding the daily operations of the CDL. The following are the standards and criteria for selecting projects:

- Strategic Applicability: Addresses a priority academic concern of the CSU and is consistent with the purpose and values of the Integrated Technology Strategy.
- Quality and Quantity of Learning: Has a high probability of improving the quality of learning in clearly definable ways, and/or will increase access to learning opportunities for a significant number of learners.
- Scalability: Is planned and developed once, is shared or implemented on multiple campuses, and is adaptable for use by multiple disciplines.
- Sustainability: Can be supported through existing, stable sources of funding and approval processes, and can deal effectively with the problems of technical obsolescence and need for continuous quality improvement.
- Resource Leveraging: Uses new funding as a means of attracting additional investment from other sources, for example, redeployment of institutional resources, grants, fund raising. (*Note:* normal operating expenditures historically associated with continuing aspects of the project do not qualify as leverage for this purpose.)
- Multicampus Participation: Involves significant, active participation of persons from multiple campuses in planning, implementing, managing, and evaluating project activities.
- Timely Results: Provides early and continuous, measurable benefits.
- Feasibility: Can be accomplished within existing institutional, technological, and financial needs and constraints, including timeframe and potential growth.
- Acceptance: Can be implemented in a way that provides for ongoing discussion and validation of the approach taken.
- Accountability: Provides academic, operational, and financial measures and metrics for monitoring the achievement of the project's objectives and outcomes.

The two criteria that are most difficult to achieve are scalability and sustainability. These are often not addressed in projects that are funded by institutions in higher education, yet they are critical to the long-term return on investments that are made by the university system. Institutions make regular and substantial investments in the development of instructional technology, yet they have problems producing high-quality instructional technology in a timely and reliable manner, and providing evidence of improvements in teaching and learning. These immediate barriers of individuals and institutions trying to implement technology enhanced education have made it more difficult to plan strategies for long-term sustainability and scalability of the discovery, creation, collection, organization, and delivery of digital learning materials.

By providing the Planning Assumptions, Planning Principles and Standards, and Criteria for Selecting Projects, the ITS planning process has created a working environment that sets the direction without locking its users into an inflexible plan of action. By focusing on the direction, and having a clear understanding of the underlying assumptions and needs, it is possible to maintain flexibility throughout the life of a project. This flexibility allows the CDL to leverage resources whenever the opportunity arises and avoids the trappings associated with more traditional planning.

Within this context, the CDL is working on three major projects: The Scalable and Sustainable Software Development project, the Multimedia Educational Resource for Learning and Online Teaching project (MERLOT), and the Community of Academic Technology Staff (CATS) project.

THE SCALABLE AND SUSTAINABLE SOFTWARE DEVELOPMENT PROJECT

The CDL was given the task of identifying the specific problems that the Multimedia Repository Initiative and the Distributed Learning and Teaching Initiative would address, along with developing an implementation strategy. The research was done within the context of the current operation of the CSU. The desired outcome was to find ways to increase the quantity of quality, Web-based teaching and learning materials.

Most universities within the CSU support faculty development of Web-based teaching and learning materials, but nearly all the work is being done in a "cottage industry" (Hanley, Schneebeck, and Zweier, 1998) that has the following characteristics:

- Development is undertaken by a single faculty member.
- The software is designed to meet the needs of the individual faculty member's course.
- Faculty software developers often don't take the time to articulate learning objectives and teaching strategies for their product.
- The primary resource devoted to the project is the faculty member's own time.
- The software developed is often designed for a specific hardware platform.

When the activity of the "cottage industry" is evaluated in the context of the CDL Standards and Criteria for Selecting Projects, it is clear that the current approach is inadequate. Individual faculty members seldom choose or can support a project that has strategic value to a campus, let alone a system. Mechanisms for evaluating the quality of the materials being produced are usually lacking. Scalability and sustainability are not achieved because individuals lack the necessary resources. Individuals are rarely in a position to leverage the work of others within their campus or system.

Although most materials developed by faculty suffered from these problems, the CDL identified a project that seemed to be quite successful. Dr. Robert Desharnais from California State University, Los Angeles, had funding from the National Science Foundation to produce Web-based biology labs. His initial prototype was being used widely by educators across the country. But he was faced with the problem of sustaining the product. The CDL agreed to work with him to develop a model to scale and sustain not only his prototype, but also 11 additional labs online.

Biology faculty from fourteen campuses of the CSU spent two days identifying critical areas of need for introductory biology labs. They identified the scientific process as a critical part of the course, but a difficult one to teach. The group agreed to create a series of biology laboratory simulations that would make it necessary for students to go through the scientific process. They choose simulations in part because they can be used in many different teaching and learning environments simply by changing the assignment that is used with them. In the process of making these decisions, the faculty had identified a project that addresses a strategic issue in the CSU, had a plan for materials that increase the quality and quantity of learning and is scalable across multiple courses. The group agreed to make the first prototype of the CDL project a laboratory simulation on evolution. This allowed the students to design and run experiments that could not possibly be done in a traditional laboratory.

Going from Case Study to Model

Developing biology simulations became a case study for the CDL to create a model for scalable and sustainable software development. Doing the project required the CDL to solve problems, and the solutions became strategies that were generalized to future projects. The CDL followed the four phases of the life-cycle development process, which are briefly discussed, and Figure 7.2 illustrates how these phases were sequenced within CDL projects.

Concept exploration phase is the first step in the development process and its focus is on validating users' needs for the software product and developing partnerships to design prototypes. The concept exploration phase involves recognizing institutional needs and developing a consensus on the strategic areas.

Demonstration and validation phase is the second step in the development process and its focus is on developing proof that the concepts can be real solutions. That is, prototypes are developed and tested to produce evidence that the proposed solution has promise for success.

Detailed design and construction phase is the third step and its focus is on developing proof that the products work well. The detailed design and con-

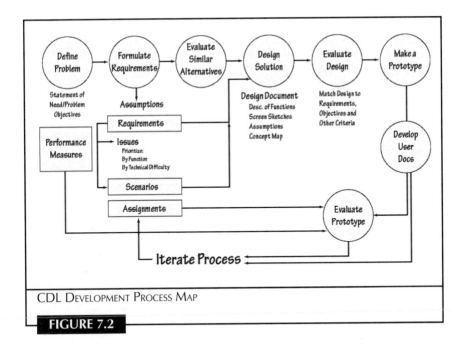

CDL DEVELOPMENT PROCESS MAP

FIGURE 7.2

struction phase involves defining all software requirements and integrating all elements rather than just the high priority elements used for developing the prototype.

Production and operation phase is the fourth step and its focus is on deploying, sustaining, and revising valued products.

The CDL's scalable and sustainable model analyzes all phases of the life-cycle development process to ensure that plans will result in successful outcomes. Although each life-cycle phase focuses on a limited set of concerns, each phase is also informed by important issues from the other life-cycle phases. Projects often cycle back through earlier phases and sometimes phases can occur in parallel. For example, the distribution and support services critical for the successful operation of the product should be considered in the earliest concept exploration phase.

To ensure life-cycle success, there are critical support processes. For each phase of a product's life cycle, the following four processes are implemented.

1. *Validation Processes: Are we solving the right problem?* The group of biology faculty identified the right problem to solve through their discussions, based on their experiences. Validating the problem throughout the life cycle is critical because the original and validated goals of the software can be easily forgotten or transformed by a focus on technology.

2. Verification Processes: Are we solving the problem right? Defining the right
goals is critical, but regularly evaluating if the goals are being achieved is
another critical process. The CDL's simulations had to be evaluated to see if
faculty could teach and students could learn the complex and dynamic concepts of biology more successfully. The CDL applied usability testing, which
provides a set of methodologies for evaluating software (and other products).
Usability is characterized by four aspects: effectiveness of the technology to
achieve the users' goals, ease of learning to use the technology by new users,
ease of using the technology by trained users, and preference for using the
technology.

Both validation and verification processes are performed at each stage of a
product's life cycle. The CDL has collaborated with the Center for Usability in
Design and Assessment (CUDA) at CSU, Long Beach (www.csulb.edu/~cuda)
to provide extensive support of both validation and verification services. The
CDL standards and criteria for selecting projects are also critical in evaluating
if the products are being developed right.

*3. Partnership Development: Do we have the right people to produce the right
product right?* All the activities and processes required to implement the scalable and sustainable model require teams of people who have to coordinate
their skills. The CDL recruited team members from the CSU campuses and
from industry. Figure 7.3 illustrates how CDL project teams are organized, with
a small core group surrounded by different levels of expertise to ensure the
success of the core group.

Finding the right people for the working groups is critical and the CDL has
been very successful in establishing partnerships with commercial publishers.
Addison-Wesley Longman (AWL) is such a commercial publisher and is a
partner with the CDL in developing and distributing a suite of Web-based
biology labs. The CDL recognized that the universities are highly skilled at the
conceptual and demonstration phase of online curriculum development, but
are progressively less capable of reliable and high-quality performance in the
detailed design, product, and operations phases. The CDL also recognized that
the commercial publishers' capabilities were complementary of the universities;
publishers were very capable of reliable and high-quality performance in the
latter life-cycle phases but were highly dependent on academia for the conceptual development and validation of curriculum. The CDL developed a business
plan to reflect the complementary nature of the partnership, and this partnership has successfully produced 12 high-quality simulations of core biological
curriculum in a 12-month period.

4. Management Processes: How do we facilitate and monitor the project? The
life-cycle phases, supporting processes, and people must be effectively coordinated. The CDL's management processes provide (a) efficient and effective
communication, (b) work environments that complement the team's work, (c)

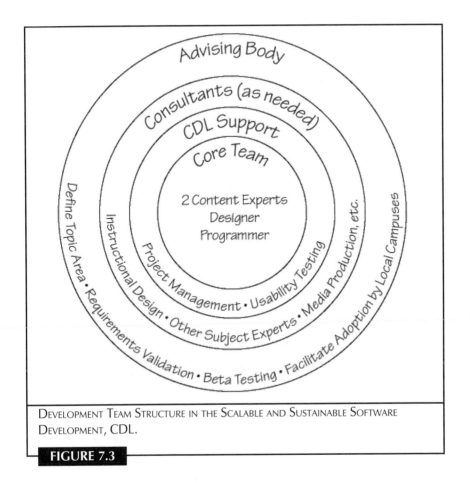

DEVELOPMENT TEAM STRUCTURE IN THE SCALABLE AND SUSTAINABLE SOFTWARE DEVELOPMENT, CDL.

FIGURE 7.3

personnel processes for acquiring, integrating, and terminating the human resources for projects, (d) effective management, funding, and scheduling for the entire life cycle of the project, and (e) quality assurance processes.

While organizing the right groups of people to construct the right product right, the CDL developed a variety of strategies to compensate people for their work and used a variety of funding resources. Faculty content experts are compensated in proportion to their contributions with royalties, release time from teaching, or stipends for work overload. Managers and staff are funded in accordance with the level of effort for specific tasks or in proportion to the institutional workload. The funding sources have included NSF grants, CDL's operating budget, CSU project funds, and AWL business contributions.

In summary, the CDL's scalable and sustainable instructional software development model provides a methodology to help decide if the right people are producing the right product right. Each step in the life-cycle development process explicitly or implicitly requires a decision by one or more teams. The project and program management processes must ensure timely as well as comprehensive decisions that include the input and acceptance by the team members. As in any organization, good people make for good work, and the CDL was fortunate to get the right blend of people with the skill sets required to get the jobs done well.

Faculty Development Is Critical for Success of Technology

Integrating instructional software into academic programs requires faculty choosing the software and knowing how to use it. Developing the faculty's skills in choosing and using instructional software became part of the CDL's model. Learning by doing, learning by using, and learning by listening were the three strategies employed.

Learning by Doing

Developing high-quality, Web-accessible learning and teaching materials is the "doing" by which the faculty learn to enhance their knowledge and skills. Faculty who are involved in the development of CDL products learn by designing the software, creating the learning assignments to turn the use of the software into effective learning experiences, and evaluating the quality of the learning materials. The intensive and collaborative involvement in a CDL project challenges the faculty's assumptions and principles of teaching and learning and provides an environment to reflect on the creation of "best practices." The reliable outcome of these challenges is that faculty realize that Web-based, modular simulations are critical to the best practice in teaching and learning. The simulations should:

- Use multimedia to comprehensively represent difficult learning problems.
- Be used by students as tools to solve problems, test hypotheses, and think critically.
- Be able to be used in a variety of ways, within a variety of curriculums, by a variety of students and teachers.

If these criteria are not satisfied, then instructional software will not be high-quality, easily accessible teaching-learning materials. It is important to note that accessible is not only defined by the technological ability to get the information, but also the human ability to understand and learn the information that is accessed.

Learning by Using

A very small percentage of the teaching faculty has the opportunity to be intensively and collaboratively developed through the design of CDL's products and processes. The planning assumption of "few develop and many use" resulted in a strategy in which faculty development occurs through the learning to use instructional technology. To this end, the CDL continues to conduct workshops to help faculty learn how to:

- Use MERLOT.
- Use the biology lab simulations.
- Develop learning assignments for online teaching resources.
- Evaluate the usability of online teaching learning materials (including their own).

These workshops are conducted by CDL staff and the faculty involved in the design of the simulations. In all the workshops, the project-based, learner-centered approach is employed. To decide how and why to use instructional technology, the faculty have to articulate learning objectives for their courses, reasons why their students are having difficulty learning certain topics, and strategies for improving student learning. In the workshops, faculty also learn to evaluate if the instructional technology is effective in achieving learning objectives, easy to learn for new users, easy to use for experienced users, and motivating to learn (the four dimensions of usability). Assessments of the workshop have indicated that significant faculty development occurs when learning to use instructional technology. For example, 47 faculty and staff from 15 different disciplines and seven different campuses participated in two-day workshops on usability testing. The following findings represent a sample of the results based on a 50% return rate of a survey.

Questions	Percentage of YES Responses
Did the workshop significantly help you develop and apply basic skills in usability testing (such as user needs assessments, heuristic evaluations, or laboratory usability testing)?	100%
Did the workshop significantly help you understand how to create an effective learning environment for your students?	100%
Did the workshop significantly help you reflect on your own teaching processes and consider new activities to enhance your teaching?	100%
Do you feel prepared to share the lessons you've learned concerning usability testing methods and outcomes,	100%

Questions	Percentage of YES Responses
and/or other practical advice that could benefit your faculty and staff colleagues?	
Do you feel that the workshop brought you and your colleagues together in ways that promoted enthusiasm and positively motivated you to work on multimedia projects that advanced your professional and/or personal development?	100%

Learning by Listening

The CDL staff regularly make presentations at academic technology conferences to disseminate information about MERLOT, the simulations, and CDL's processes for developing instructional technology. Conferences are a key mechanism for marketing CDL's products and processes.

In summary, the CDL scalable and sustainable model was developed by solving the specific problems in building simulations, using systems engineering and instructional design principles to guide the problem solving and reflecting on the success and scalability of the processes. Constantly keeping focused on the teaching-learning problem was critical for the success of the biology evolution lab case study and for creating a model that resulted in the development of many other simulations.

THE MULTIMEDIA EDUCATIONAL RESOURCE FOR LEARNING AND ONLINE TEACHING PROJECT (MERLOT)

Two major challenges facing higher education are accessibility to and usability of high-quality, Web-based, interactive learning materials. The promises of digital learning materials actively engaging students and teachers in effective education have been met with faculty experiencing difficulty in finding relevant digital materials; evaluating the quality of their content, potential efficacy in teaching and learning, usability, and stability; integrating the materials into a comprehensive pedagogical context that meets the needs of their students; overcoming the traditional isolation of teaching to seek advice from other faculty about the operation, uses, and assessment of digital materials; and overcoming the additional time and workload demands currently required to integrate technology into their students' learning.

Since 1997, the CDL has developed and provided free access to MERLOT (www.merlot.org) which is an open source collection of over 4,000 Web-based learning materials. MERLOT is a derivative of the NSF funded project "Authoring Tools and an Educational Object Economy." The learning materials are modules (learning objects) that faculty can integrate into their curriculum and pedagogy in ways that meet the learning and teaching needs of students and faculty. The collection is a multifaceted searchable database of URLs for learning materials that have descriptions and can have expert peer-reviews, learning assignments, user comments, technical tips, and IMS metadata attached. The URLs are automatically checked each week to ensure their availability and operability. The MERLOT collection is also a searchable database of MERLOT member profiles, which contains information about the member's areas of expertise (subject area and technical), projects, and contributions to MERLOT.

The collections are expanding for any person who registers as a member. This open source approach is designed to transform a repository into a dynamic online community. The collection of learning materials and member profiles are tools to enable teachers and learners to become participants in the MERLOT online community. The sharing and reviewing of learning materials, posting news and events, and connecting the learning materials and people to one's own endeavors create a community of users, in which an individual's efforts benefit a multitude of people.

The design of the MERLOT software has been driven by a user-centered approach that enables effective use of and access to the collection by users and contributors. The collection provides easy access to learning materials and human resources to improve education. Current usage rates for MERLOT average over 235,000 hits per month (March 2001).

To support the effective integration of MERLOT into university teaching and learning, the CDL has designed and delivered faculty development programs. Usability testing of MERLOT and assessment of its faculty development programs have been important, ongoing activities supporting the continuous improvement of MERLOT.

In 1998, a State Higher Education Executive Officers/American Productivity and Quality Center (SHEEO/APQC) benchmarking study on faculty development and instructional technology selected the CDL as one of the nation's six best practices centers. This selection initiated a collaboration among the CSU, University of Georgia System, Oklahoma State Regents for Higher Education, and University of North Carolina System, creating a consortium representing almost 100 campuses serving over 900,000 students and over 47,000 faculty.

In 1999, the four systems recognized the significant benefits of a cooperative initiative to expand the MERLOT collections, conduct peer reviews of the digital learning materials, and add student learning assignments. Each system contributed $20,000 in cash and over $30,000 in in-kind support to advance the collaborative project. The CSU maintained its leadership of and responsibilities for the operation and improvement of processes and tools, and SHEEO became the coordinator for the cooperative of the four state systems.

As the complexity of the collaboration significantly increased with the recruitment of an additional 19 system/consortia members to the MERLOT project, it was recognized that the scope of coordination activities had gone beyond the mission and capability of SHEEO and a new, neutral coordinating organization needed to be established. To that end, MERLOT.org was established as a nonprofit organization and its organizational infrastructure is currently being developed and will advance the current collaborative framework. The CSU will continue to provide the core operational products and services for the digital collection, user-interface, and peer review processes.

The 23 higher education institutions, state systems, and consortia currently within the MERLOT project are implementing the peer review of digital materials in the disciplines of biology, business, physics, teacher education, chemistry, world languages, health sciences, history, information technology, mathematics, music, and psychology. The activities for this project are based on the experiences acquired over the past two years and formal assessment of the peer review project. The 23 participants in MERLOT for fiscal year 2000–2001 are:

Association of Jesuit Colleges and Universities—Distance Education Network
Board of Regents, State of Iowa
California Community College System
California State University
Canadian CAREO Project (Universities of Alberta and Calgary)
Canadian COHERE Project (Universities of Alberta, Guelph, Waterloo, and York University)
Council of Independent Colleges, Foundation for Independent Higher Education, and National Association of Independent Colleges and Universities
Florida Virtual Campus
Illinois Board of Higher Education
Indiana Commission for Higher Education
Louisiana Board of Regents
Oklahoma State Regents for Higher Education
South Dakota Board of Regents
State University of New York
Tennessee Board of Regents and University of Tennessee
Troy State University
University of Hawaii
University of Michigan
University of North Carolina
University System of Georgia
University of Wisconsin System

Virginia Community College System

Western Cooperative for Educational Telecommunications (representing Universities of Utah, Nevada-Las Vegas, Wyoming, Arizona State University, Community Colleges of Colorado, Weber State University, and the University of Alaska System)

The MERLOT project will leverage the academic culture of scholarship and research and the academic administration culture of higher education institutions to engage faculty and their discipline communities in the scholarship of teaching. The peer-review process will help ensure that learning materials address significant theoretical or research issues and are contextually accurate, pedagogically sound, and technically easy to use.

Quality Assurance

Developing Evaluation Standards. Defining the qualities of "good" digital learning materials is critical for a peer-review process to conduct reliable and valid evaluations. Three categories of evaluation standards have been used by the current MERLOT discipline communities and will be the framework used in future communities; each discipline community will have to operationalize these categories for use within their discipline. The three general categories of evaluation standards are Quality of Content, Potential Effectiveness as a Teaching-Learning Tool, and Ease of Use.

Quality of Content. There are two general elements to quality of content. First, do the learning materials present valid (correct) concepts, models, and skills? To evaluate the validity of the content, the reviewers will rely on their expertise. Second, do the learning materials present educationally significant concepts, models, and skills for the discipline? To evaluate the educational significance of the content, reviewers decide if the content is core curriculum within the discipline, difficult to teach and learn, and/or is a prerequisite for understanding more advanced material in the discipline.

Potential Effectiveness for Teaching and Learning. Determining actual effectiveness requires actual use of the digital learning materials by students and faculty and the systematic assessment of outcomes. Evaluating *potential* effectiveness asks the reviewers to judge, based on their expertise as teachers, if the digital materials are likely to improve teaching and learning given the ways the faculty and students could use them. The reviewers are provided with an established set of principles of effective learner-centered education developed by the American Psychology Association along with MERLOT guidelines and any discipline-specific guidelines. This evaluation dimension is conditional on how the digital learning materials are used.

Ease of Use. The basic question underlying the ease of use standard is, "How easy is it for teachers and students to use the digital learning materials for the first time?" A summary of usability heuristics is provided as a guideline.

Applying Evaluation Standards Within A Peer-review Process

Although faculty are familiar with the peer review of research and scholarship within their field, the peer review of instructional technology is new. MERLOT provides workshops for faculty to develop discipline-specific evaluation standards for digital learning materials and to develop and practice processes for conducting peer review of digital learning materials. Integrity in the peer-review process is critical for this project. Consequently, the discipline groups develop substantial inter-rater reliability in the evaluation of sample digital learning materials before the peer review process is implemented on a larger collection. Three different faculty who have relevant expertise review each learning material. Faculty reviewers write peer-review reports then send the reports to the discipline leader who integrates them into a single peer-review report.

The peer review report contains a description of the learning goals, targeted student population(s), prerequisite knowledge/skills, type of learning material, summary of procedures for using the software, and technical requirements; an evaluation and observations on the quality of the content, potential effectiveness as a teaching-learning tool, and ease of use of the materials; and comments and recommendations provided only for the author. An important feature of the peer-review process is that the authors of the learning materials are provided comprehensive and specific feedback. Consequently, the peer reviews not only help users select good materials but also aid authors to improve their materials.

Complementing Peer Reviews with User Comments

The peer-review process of digital learning materials is designed to inherit and improve on the validity and reliability of the evaluation processes present in the peer review of scholarship. The process also inherits some of the constraints of the scholarship model, such as timeliness of reviews, potential biases created by the selection of a small set of reviewers, and limited evaluation standards.

MERLOT has a second and parallel review process that complements the formal peer reviews. Anyone who signs up as an individual member of MERLOT can contribute user comments. The user-centered review process has precedence in a number of highly used Web sites, such as Amazon.com, and allows individuals to provide their observations and evaluations on the learning materials within MERLOT. A user comments page is connected to every learning material and has guidelines for feedback. Quality of content, potential effectiveness as a teaching-learning tool, and ease of use are some of the areas for comments. User comments can also contain information about student learning outcomes. Finally, users can comment on the learning assignments, peer reviews, technical tips, or other particulars connected with the learning materials.

Creating Communities to Conduct Reviews

MERLOT started with state institutions of higher education as the initial collaborators for implementing peer-review processes rather than professional disciplinary organizations. The benefits of starting with higher education institutions are: institutions have the responsibility and the faculty for delivering high-quality teaching and learning (most professional organizations' primary focus is on research and scholarship); institutions provide the resources and infrastructure for faculty to develop and contribute digital learning materials (professional organizations might provide guidelines and evaluations, but not resources for the development of the materials themselves); and institutions have the financial resources and accountability concerns that can mobilize a large number of faculty to perform the work (professional organizations do not have such resources). These assumptions guided the strategy for using institutions of higher education in first establishing discipline communities of reviewers and then transitioning the responsibility to the professional discipline organizations.

The CDL has developed a framework for institutions of higher education to collaborate on the MERLOT project. The framework is outlined in an application for participation and includes a $25,000 membership contribution, the appointment of an institutional project director, and the set of services provided to the systems by the MERLOT project (see http://taste.merlot.org for details). The project directors are given guidelines for their roles within MERLOT, serve on an advisory board, and are the primary communication link between the MERLOT project and the institutional participant.

Project directors select and provide support for faculty for the discipline communities developing and conducting the peer review of digital learning materials. The support for faculty includes travel to MERLOT meetings and stipends or release time for their efforts. The selection criteria for faculty reviewers are: recognized expertise in the discipline, recognized excellence in teaching, experience using (and/or developing) technology in teaching and learning, and meaningful participation in activities of professional discipline associations.

MERLOT discipline communities also have faculty leaders who facilitate the development and productivity of the faculty reviewers. In addition to the four criteria for reviewers, discipline leaders have demonstrated skills in facilitating groups and project management. The discipline leaders are supported with monthly teleconferences to identify and resolve issues, monitor progress of communities' activities, and assess needs for tools and processes to enable the communities' success.

Tools and Processes for Peer Review

The face-to-face MERLOT workshops are critical for establishing the professional and personal sense of community through the consensual development of evaluation standards and peer-review processes that serve each discipline. To sustain and enhance this sense of community and ensure the virtual communities' productivity and continued development as a discipline community, Web-based worksites were designed to support the asynchronous work and communication among the members of the MERLOT project. These Web-based worksites have been tested and implemented in the current MERLOT activities. There are four levels of communication tools within MERLOT that sustain and enhance the discipline communities' implementation of the peer-review process.

MERLOT public Web sites are the MERLOT-Central Web site and the MERLOT-Discipline Web sites. The MERLOT-Central Web site provides access to browse and advanced search tools for the entire collection. The MERLOT-Discipline Web sites are modifications of the MERLOT-Central functionality and interfaces that meet the specific and developing requirements of the discipline. Both public Web sites contain a repository of the URL addresses and descriptions for teaching-learning materials, profiles of people within the MERLOT community, documents about the peer-review processes, and communication tools.

MERLOT Internal Discipline Web site is a password-protected gateway to worksites for the faculty who are sponsored by the MERLOT institutional participants. This Web site contains sections for each discipline group to post documents, access the discipline's listserv, and participate in the group's threaded discussion. The password protection will provide the discipline communities with a safe working environment to reflect on their work so that they can produce the highest quality outcome for public consumption the first time it is posted on the MERLOT public Web site. As the peer-review culture and discipline communities mature, direct interdisciplinary interactions will be encouraged.

MERLOT Internal Coordination Web site is a password-protected Web site similar to the internal discipline site that enables the MERLOT institutional project directors, the discipline leaders, and the CDL staff to post documents, enter the listserv, and participate in threaded discussions. The purpose of this Web site is to review the documents, tools, and processes designed for the discipline communities and MERLOT organization before they go out to the faculty groups, ensuring high-quality and consistent communication.

MERLOT Internal CSU Administration Web site is the workspace for the CSU-CDL to develop and review the tools, templates, and processes before they are distributed to the internal coordination Web site.

Sustaining the Peer-review Processes

Over time, the MERLOT discipline community will have the normal transitions of leadership and reviewers, and the changing personnel is a significant risk to the sustainability of the peer-review process. If the tools, processes, decisions, and discussions are not captured for others to use, the discipline community could become disabled by the loss of critical personnel. Another risk is that new people joining the community need to be quickly acculturated or they could impede the momentum, misunderstand the processes, be counterproductive, and/or drop out. The public and internal Web sites are critical for reducing these risks. These Web sites are archives that capture much information on the discipline communities and enable the discipline communities to sustain themselves while individual members transition in and out of the organization.

Establishing the discipline peer-review committees, providing the evaluation standards and training, and managing the peer-review process will initially be coordinated by the CDL. To sustain the peer-review process, the responsibility for directing the review process will transfer to professional discipline organization(s) whose mission includes defining the standards for and continuously improving teaching and learning within the discipline. Professional discipline organizations have been responsible for the development, validation, dissemination, and at times accreditation of the scholarly and instructional standards for the discipline. Universities and the culture of the discipline have accepted this important role of the professional organizations and use their reviews in curriculum planning, program revisions, funding decisions, and retention, tenure, and promotion decisions.

The mutual dependencies among universities who employ faculty to advance and teach the discipline and the professional organizations that define the standards for teaching and advances in research and scholarship are at the core of the MERLOT project's framework. What the MERLOT project provides is a working process for the peer review of digital learning materials that directly benefits both higher education institutions and professional discipline organizations. Accepted evaluation standards by professional organizations can be used by higher education institutions to guide their selection, support, and evaluation of academic technology in ways that complement the peer-review of scholarship and curriculum content of academic programs.

Developing associations with the discipline's professional organization will be led by the discipline leaders and faculty reviewers (professional affiliation was one of the selection criteria). Representatives from professional organizations will meet with members of the MERLOT project to develop the goals, strategies, and requirements for engaging professional organizations in the peer-review process. At this interdisciplinary meeting, the professional discipline organizations, MERLOT discipline leaders, and the CDL will develop processes that will become models for other disciplines. The plans for the professional organizations are to revise and approve the evaluation standards for digital learning materials for their discipline, disseminate these standards at their professional meetings, solicit reviewers, select materials to be reviewed, and coordinate the writing of review reports. Figure 7.4 illustrates the transition process.

A critical aspect of getting the professional organizations to accept and fulfill the peer-review responsibilities is that the authors of digital learning materials will have the opportunity to have their scholarship of teaching be recognized by authoritative organizations in their discipline. If professional organizations accept the responsibilities, then the university retention, tenure, and promotion processes can be leveraged to motivate faculty to make contributions to the scholarship of teaching with digital materials. Faculty teaching with digital material identified as high-quality by their discipline can also receive recognition within their retention, tenure, and promotion processes for high-quality instructional practices.

MERLOT is also working with EDUCAUSE, a leading professional organization focusing on technology in higher education, to support a national forum

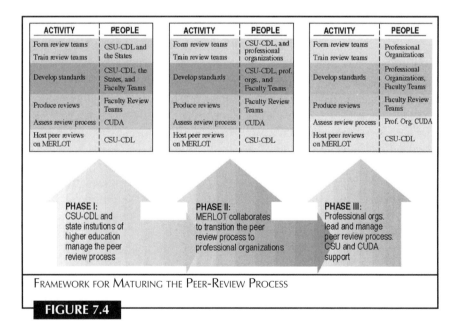

FRAMEWORK FOR MATURING THE PEER-REVIEW PROCESS

FIGURE 7.4

for sharing lessons learned from the MERLOT project. Enabling professional organizations to reliably validate the quality of digital learning materials within their disciplines is a critical step for sustaining the peer-review process and making it adaptable to a wide range of digital collection providers and valuable for users.

Leveraging Resources for Success

The CDL is pursuing both sponsors (entities that pay for a presence on a Web site to build goodwill and brand recognition) and partners (entities that actively engage with MERLOT to deliver products and/or services) to help sustain the MERLOT project. The organized MERLOT collection of academic content with its connected peer reviews and pedagogical resources is a powerful tool that enhances the value of academic technology products, both commercial and noncommercial.

Course management tools (such as Blackboard, eCollege, TopClass, and WebCT) are user-friendly templates that enable faculty to organize and monitor digital materials and communications in a Web-based environment. One of the barriers to optimally using these tools is the faculty's access to high-quality, reliably accessible academic content. MERLOT can provide access to academic content that would enhance the value of the course management tools and the course management tools would enhance the value of MERLOT because the academic content could be easily organized by faculty into their own specific curriculum. Leveraging the complementary nature of MERLOT (and other digital collections) and course management tools is a win–win strategy for MERLOT and course management tool companies.

Partnerships will be one strategy to address the unreliable access to high-quality learning materials. The "cottage industry" for developing digital learning materials has produced some excellent instructional materials, but when user demands exceed server capabilities, the materials become functionally inaccessible. Hosting these high-quality, frequently used materials on centrally supported, operated, and maintained servers is one strategy being pursued by the CDL. Partnerships among authors, private sector companies, and the MERLOT project would be one mechanism for sustaining this type of activity.

Predicted Impact of MERLOT

The development and implementation of a sustainable, scalable, and high-quality peer review of digital learning materials is a critical element for excellence in higher education. The collaboration of institutions of higher education and professional organizations within the MERLOT project provides a unique and powerful mechanism for achieving this excellence. The impact of the peer-review processes within the MERLOT project will occur in these areas:

Advances in the community of higher education institutions

- Learning to collaborate rather than compete provides a significant advantage for institutions. Even the largest university systems recognize that they cannot develop all the high-quality, interactive, usable, and reusable digital learning materials needed to support excellence in their academic programs.

- Directly connecting professional organizations with the review of teaching-learning materials provides institutions reliable assessments of their investments in developing technology-enhanced curriculum.

Advances in discipline-specific and general education

- The peer review of digital learning materials brings together the inseparable elements of excellent education: quality content, pedagogical soundness, and student-centered delivery.

- Sharing educationally sound teaching-learning materials and pedagogy will significantly serve the needs of newly hired faculty, whose training in research far exceeds their training in teaching. The "secrets" of good teaching can be shared so students and faculty can benefit from good practices.

- The peer-review processes and reports create valid and reliable methods for evaluating the growing scholarship of teaching with technology. Faculty's significant and critical investment in discipline-specific curriculum development can be appropriately recognized through the peer-review process.

The broad impact of the proposed peer-review process and MERLOT project can be achieved because of the well-managed, user-centered, collaborative framework that defines the MERLOT project. The importance of developing a scalable and sustainable model is critical to achieving lasting and significant advances in higher education.

In summary, the MERLOT project will result in faculty and students being able to find and identify high-quality digital learning materials quickly and easily. By reading the attached peer-review and user comments, students and faculty will know that the simulation, tutorial, or other digital item is reliable, usable, and valuable. Faculty seeking materials to enhance lessons and/or develop curriculum will have access to a collection of excellent resources. And the efforts of faculty who create, develop, contribute, and review the digital learning materials will contribute to the scholarship of teaching model. The success of this project will affect higher education in a lasting, powerful way. The potential impact of this project is enormous.

THE COMMUNITY OF ACADEMIC TECHNOLOGY STAFF PROJECT (CATS)

The Scalable and Sustainable Software project and the MERLOT project are resulting in the increase of quality Web-based teaching and learning materials. Yet as these projects succeed, the demand for academic technology support staff continues to grow. Given the political and financial realities of most universities, it is not likely that sufficient new staff will be hired to meet the demand. The question becomes: can the issues of scalability be addressed for academic technology support staff by modifying their working environment? Another version of the same question: how can staff become more productive with relatively stable funding and without massive burnout?

These difficult questions were being addressed in some manner on each campus, but the only significant conversation about these issues among campuses was happening among managers. The intellectual capital of the staff was not being tapped in any kind of an organized manner. In the CSU system, the staff is distributed across the campuses and often must provide their own training and problem solving. The CDL took on the challenge of finding a way to tap the intellectual capital of the staff to identify strategic issues and explore ways to address the problems.

The CDL is supporting a Community of Academic Technology Staff (CATS) that provides an environment for the sharing of resources and information and thus reduces the need for every staff member to solve all problems from scratch. CATS exchange their expertise through the yearly CATS conference, as well as the CATS online community.

In 1998, the CDL sponsored the first annual CATS Conference. The CDL provided project management support for the event, but the entire program was planned by staff, for staff. The CDL provided funding for four staff members from each of the 23 campuses to attend the conference. Other staff and managers were welcome to attend, but were required to pay their own expenses. The response was overwhelming. One hundred twenty people attended the conference, and good things happened. They met their counterparts from other campuses. They had an opportunity to show off their best work to their colleagues, and described the way their "shops" were organized. They had meals together and shared an evening of entertainment. It was the first significant step in creating a community.

During the conference there were several sessions at which the staff were asked to identify some of the problems that they faced in their daily work environments. Their responses included:

- A constant demand for more support than they could deliver.

- Insufficient time to learn new products and procedures that are necessary to provide quality support.

- Insufficient time to develop the necessary training tools and templates.

- Lack of reliable evaluations of new hardware and software products.

The CDL recognized the potential that, after the conference, the staff would return to their workplace, get busy putting out fires, and very little would change. In an attempt to give the conference some lasting value, the participants were introduced to MERLOT. They were encouraged to post training tools and templates along with other resources that had been developed by the staff of the CSU to address some of the time problems associated with creating these tools.

Within two years, over 108 technical tools were posted on MERLOT. They include tools for software training, laboratory management, specialized software applications, faculty support, and Web page design. These resources are shared not only by the academic technology staff of the CSU, but by staff from around the world. Because MERLOT encourages participation from any interested party, about one-third of the technical tools are from staff from outside the CSU.

The CDL also agreed to sponsor a series of systemwide videoconferences in which the staff would address topics of common concern. Videoconferences supported by the CDL include: using WebCT, instructional design: micro and macro perspectives; online databases: tools, projects, issues for CSU staff; and a report on CSU staff projects. The videoconferences used the videoconferencing network of the CSU, and over 300 staff members were involved.

Now the CDL sponsors an annual CATS conference. Participation has grown to over 160 staff members, and is expected to continue to grow. Members of CATS are preparing a MERLOT community of interest that will allow academic technology staff from around the world to exchange tools, ideas, hardware and software reviews, and to have asynchronous communications. Sharing these materials through the MERLOT CATS has the potential of increasing the effectiveness of existing staff by reducing the time they must spend doing all these activities. Through the professional development and support of academic technology staff, faculty are provided highly trained technical support that is critical for translating academic ideas into viable instructional technology.

FINAL COMMENTS

The fundamental keys to the scalable and sustainable success of the CDL are cooperation and understanding the readiness and goals of individual and institutional users of technology.

MERLOT, CATS, and the Scalable and Sustainable Model all require the sharing of expertise and resources. The win–win cooperation creates an environment that encourages grassroots participation. Faculty and staff become members of the communities, help build the collections of learning materials and tools, and are involved in the quality control of these materials. This enables the faculty and staff to have a larger collection of Web-based learning materials and technical tools to choose from as they develop and deliver courses. The faculty remain in control of the teaching and learning process and staff are empowered with tools.

The projects of the CDL address strategic issues that may require institutional change to be most effective. But the CDL does not advocate that faculty or institutions radically change the way they do their work as the first step. Instead it creates an environment that facilitates faculty who want to use new tools and pedagogies to improve teaching and learning. The CDL does not attempt to create policy or take on issues such as ownership of intellectual property. For instance, when working with publishers, the traditional book model where faculty receive a royalty for their work is used. Change happens in incremental steps, and it happens to faculty, staff, and administrators because they see an advantage to changing the way they work and learn.

The number of people willing to share learning materials and training tools continues to grow. There is good evidence that many faculty and staff are quite willing to become involved in Web-based communities, and the CDL will continue its work to create more robust communities.

REFERENCES

American Productivity and Quality Center Web site is: www.apqc.org.

Boyer, E. L. (1997). *Scholarship Reconsidered: Priorities of the Professoriate.* New York: Carnegie Foundation.

Desharnais, R. A. (1999). "Learning by Doing with Biology Labs On-line." *Strategies for Success,* 31, pp. 1–3.

Desharnais, R. A., and G. N. Novak. (1998). Virtual courseware for science education. *Syllabus,* 12, p. 54.

Hanley, G. L., C. Schneebeck, and L. Zweier. (1998). Implementing a scalable and sustainable model for instructional software development. *Syllabus,* 11, pp 30-34.

IMS.org, originally sponsored by EDUCAUSE and its National Learning Information Infrastructure initiative, is developing universal, open standards and technical specifications for accessing and sharing digital learning materials; the Web address is: http://www.imsproject.org/index.html.

National Research Council. *Developing a Digital National Library for SMET Education: Report of a Workshop.* Washington, DC: National Academy Press, 1998.

Nielson, J. (1993). *Usability Engineering.* Boston: Academic Press.

Nielson, J. (1994). *Usability Inspection Methods.* New York: John Wiley & Sons.

Spohrer, J., and the East/West Authoring Tools Group. (1998). *Authoring Tools and an Educational Object Economy* (NSF Grant CDA-9408607). http://www.eoe.org/events/TRPFinalReport/index.htm.

CHAPTER 8

Beyond Button-Pushing
Using Technology to Improve Learning

A. W. (Tony) Bates

INTRODUCTION

T he purpose of this chapter is to pull together the main themes that
emerge from this study of best practice with regard to faculty development in instructional technology. I am using three sources for this
analysis: the individual case studies covered in earlier chapters; a screening
survey of 35 North American universities and colleges and seven for-profit
organizations; and the APQC/SHEEO sharing session final report. This chapter draws particularly on the work of Marisa Brown and Kimberley Lopez at
APQC, who did much of the analysis of this research data.

THE SCREENING SURVEY

In Chapter 2, Marisa Brown and Ron Webb describe how the sponsor institutions at the initial planning and kick-off meeting developed a set of best-
practice criteria that was used to determine which schools, colleges, and
companies should be selected as possible candidates for site visits. This resulted
in the nomination of 80 best-practice candidates. Each of these 80 organizations was invited to complete a questionnaire (the screening survey), and 43
(54%) responded. One questionnaire was unusable, so the sample consisted of
responses from 35 universities and colleges and from seven private sector
organizations. The survey was conducted in 1998.

The main purpose of the screening survey was to select seven institutions for site visits, those that seemed from the questionnaires to be the "crème de la crème" of best practice institutions in faculty development for instructional technology. It is important to recognize that the survey sample is not a random sample, but is based on peer-group identification of institutions considered to be best practice as a result of applying commonly agreed criteria.

However, the survey does provide valuable information about what a larger sample of organizations nominated as possible candidates for good practice are doing with regard to supporting faculty development in instructional technology.

SITE VISITS

The case studies in the previous chapters of this book reflect the views of those working within the institutions visited. However, the APQC/SHEEO study was based on the observations of external observers from sponsor organizations who visited the seven selected institutions.

The site visit reports more or less followed the same organizational structure as the screening survey, based on the following headings: institutional context; teaching and learning issues; organizational issues; policies and funding; and performance measurement.

In this chapter I will try to integrate results from the screening survey, the site visit reports, and the case studies. This, of course, will reflect my own views on the findings; in particular, the conclusions drawn are my personal opinions, and not necessarily those of APQC, SHEEO, or the sponsor organizations.

CURRENT INSTITUTIONAL CONTEXT

It is important to look at the overall institutional context with regard to instructional technologies when examining faculty development. For instance, institutions without a formal commitment to the use of instructional technology in teaching and learning are less likely to have policies for faculty development in this area.

The screening survey found that of the 35 responding universities and colleges, 21 (60%) had a formal written plan or policy for the use of instructional technologies, and 12 (34%) had one under development. Only two had no formal instructional technology plan either developed or in the works. All seven of the best-practice organizations had an instructional technology plan.

In the seven best-practice institutions selected for site visits, their instructional technology plans reflected a response to pressures from the external environment, such as rapid enrollment growth, the changing educational needs of a knowledge-based workforce, and especially the need for technological literacy. Instructional technology was also seen as a major means to reach out beyond the walls of the campus and provide equal opportunities for access to higher education to all within their mandated jurisdiction. Some were also driven by the need to demonstrate to key stakeholders improved effectiveness and increased productivity, and saw instructional technology as a major means to achieve this. In one case, the move to increased use of instructional technology was a response to major cuts in operating grants from government. However, in most cases the instructional technology plans were driven more by positive than negative rationales.

The 35 universities and colleges surveyed also provided information on the basic technology infrastructure within their organizations. If faculty do not use computers in their own office, they are not likely to use them in the classroom. All 35 institutions indicated that a majority of their faculty had individual access to a personal computer and Internet access, with most of the computers having multimedia capacity and being less than five years old. Virginia Tech linked the initial allocation and then the three-year upgrading of faculty computers and networking to faculty development workshops. In other words, to get an upgrade you had to take a faculty development course. In most institutions, students were provided with a limited amount of Internet access, but students were expected to have their own computer in less than half the 35 institutions. More significantly, even in the 35 institutions considered candidates for best practice, less than half of the classrooms were equipped for multimedia use. Nevertheless, 21 (60%) of the 35 institutions claimed that technology was incorporated into instruction in more than half their classes. This suggests that many faculty are using technology for teaching, even though the classroom environment is not designed to support it.

The site visits really reinforced the finding that best practice in faculty development in instructional technology is most likely to be found in institutions that have a culture pervaded with technology. These approaches include:

- A strong instructional technology plan for the institution.

- Extensive investment in technology infrastructure.

- Support from senior leadership for the use of technology in teaching.

- Support for faculty members in terms of project funding, release time, technical support, computer upgrades, and faculty development.

- Support for students through computer access, Internet accounts, and financial support.

In other words, faculty development opportunities may be necessary, but on their own are unlikely to be sufficient to ensure widespread use of technology for teaching within an organization. Indeed, in the 35 universities and colleges in the survey, technical support and Web page development support were rated as the most urgent needs for faculty, although training in instructional methods was also identified as an important need.

Teaching and Learning Issues

Probably the most important finding from the study is that best-practice institutions keep their focus on teaching and learning issues, and not on the technology itself. Technology is a tool, a means to various ends, but rarely an end in itself.

This may appear to be a statement of the obvious, but it is something that is often forgotten, particularly by the government or private sector companies who see online learning as a set of products or tools to be sold for profit. While Web courseware such as WebCT or Blackboard are useful supports for instructors, the key issue is how best to use these tools to improve the effectiveness of teaching and learning. Virginia Tech, for instance, bases its professional development workshops on teaching issues identified by faculty members, then looks at how the use of technology may help with the identified issue.

At the same time, the study also found that faculty members must also reach a minimum comfort level with the technology before they can realize deeper educational benefits. Collège Boréal, for example, provides all faculty members with a minimum skill set in educational technology, including training in the operation of Windows, electronic communication, and the Internet.

Thus the survey indicated that 31 out of the 33 universities and colleges responding to the question reported that they offered workshops both on instructional design *and* on how to create Web pages.

Another important finding from the study centered around the course development process. Good quality technology-based teaching and learning requires a professional approach and time for planning and implementation. There are no shortcuts. The following steps to ensure high-quality teaching and learning through technology were found within each of the seven best-practice organizations:

- Needs assessment
- Project planning
- Instructional design and development
- Formative evaluation and testing
- Materials development

Despite this, faculty members tend to oppose or avoid direct instruction in instructional design. Design concepts need to emerge in response to dealing with real teaching issues rather than being taught directly to faculty. Thus faculty development initiatives in best-practice institutions are often project oriented and/or based on a team approach to the design and delivery of technology-based materials. The best-practice institutions all had systematic course development processes in place.

One of the most interesting findings to come from the survey of the 35 universities and colleges concerned the topic of how technology-based courses are designed and developed. One question was: what was the most effective strategy for developing technology-based courses at your institution? A team approach using instructional designers, graphic designers, and so on was indicated by 23 (65%) of all institutions. Another 11 institutions (32%) indicated that the best way to develop technology-based courses was an instructor working with professional technical assistance. Only one institution indicated that this was best done by an instructor working with student assistance, and none indicated that it was best done by an instructor working alone.

However, in practice, only four of the 35 institutions (12%) actually used a team approach, while in 13 institutions (37%) the instructor was solely responsible, and in another 12 institutions instructors (33%) had assistance only from students. Thus there was a wide gap between what is considered best practice and reality in most institutions. There are possibly two reasons for this. Faculty members still jealously guard their autonomy, and this is often interpreted as a desire and preference to work individually. At the same time, relatively few institutions have put in place training, support mechanisms, and rewards to encourage faculty members to work in a team. This is probably the biggest cultural change that needs to occur for the development of high-quality technology-based teaching.

Although training acquired by faculty during project development is important, nevertheless most best-practice organizations also conducted workshops and courses for faculty. For instance, the University of Central Florida offered IDL 6543, a faculty development program to prepare faculty to develop and deliver online programs. Other common topics within the 33 universities and colleges, besides instructional design and creating Web pages, were using presentation software (86%), selecting and using Web authorware (80%), matching technology to learning outcomes (77%), and using computer conferencing software (74%).

Courses and workshops were only two of many different activities undertaken by faculty in the 35 institutions surveyed. Peer group "show and tell" sessions, provision of online resources such as Web sites and online articles on instructional development, and a multimedia development studio with professional technical support were also quite common.

These findings raise the question about the best way to organize and manage faculty development for instructional technology. The clear lesson is that faculty development with regard to instructional technology needs to be integrated within the wider context of how best to teach in higher education. From the experience of these best-practice institutions, professional development with regard to instructional technology seems to work best when it is embedded in actual teaching projects. We will see in the next section that one way to ensure this is through project management.

Organizational issues

This section will deal with three issues: incentives for faculty development in instructional technology, project management, and organizational structure.

In general, most universities and colleges are still struggling with how to reward the use of technology in teaching through the formal appointment, tenure, and promotion process. Research is still the driving and sometimes only criterion, with teaching at best a poor relation. This is a difficult issue, as ultimately the criteria for appointment, tenure, and promotion are set by faculty members themselves. It will take some time before sufficient numbers of faculty have experienced the virtues and drawbacks of technology-based teaching for it to become a generally accepted criterion for appointment, tenure, and promotion.

In the meantime, best-practice organizations have adopted several other strategies for encouraging faculty development in instructional technology. Perhaps the most important is the intrinsic value faculty get from using technology for teaching. Many faculty members on the site visits mentioned that the use of technology had reinvigorated their teaching and had boosted morale. For many it was fun.

Institutions can also do a good deal to remove barriers to the use of technology for teaching. Some of the strategies suggested to encourage faculty working on technology-based teaching projects are:

- Appropriate instructional design and technical support for faculty.
- Adjustment of class workload and/or release time for developing materials.
- Clarity and fairness with regard to intellectual property, use of copyright material, and ownership of technology-based materials.
- Teaching awards.
- Provision of laptop computers to faculty.
- Unlimited Internet access from home.
- Three hours a week "blank" timetable for project development.
- Payment of fees for courses on using new technologies.

Nevertheless, while all these incentives are valuable, ultimately innovative teaching (with or without the use of technology) must become a major criterion for appointment, tenure, and promotion, if technology is to become a critical component of university and college teaching.

One common complaint from faculty members is that teaching with technology is very time consuming compared with face-to-face teaching. This is because instructional technology requires a combination of subject expertise, instructional design, graphics design, an understanding of Web and other Internet technologies, and sometimes multimedia production skills. It is really impossible to train any single person to be an expert in all these fields, and even if they were a true Renaissance person, the time needed to cover all the necessary activities would leave little time for other academic activities, such as research.

It is not surprising that most best-practice institutions put heavy emphasis on the need for teamwork to develop quality technology-based teaching. Most of the seven best-practice institutions went further than merely bringing teams of people together; they operated a system of project management, in which technology-based teaching is based on projects with fixed allocations of time, money, and resources. A project team approach avoids the need for major retraining of faculty in skills outside their subject area expertise and provides relief from technology overload by setting a boundary around the time and resources available to complete a project.

The survey of the 35 universities and colleges found a wide variety of organizational arrangements for managing faculty development. However, 20 of the 33 institutions that responded to the relevant question (61%) and most of the seven best practice institutions had a central unit that supported faculty development.

What was interesting was that most of the best-practice institutions also drew from a range of other units to support faculty development in instructional technology, such as a center for distributed learning, computer services, and the library. As a result, best-practice institutions usually had a senior manager, such as an Associate Vice-President Academic or Chief Information Officer with responsibility for coordination and liaison between the various support units with regard to faculty development in instructional technology. This again recognizes that not all the skills necessarily reside in any one operational unit.

Indeed, most of the best practice institutions operated both centralized and decentralized faculty support services in parallel. In some cases, for instance, although support staff reported to a central unit, they were located within a specific faculty or teaching department. More discussion about the balance between centralized and decentralized support units can be found in Bates (2000).

Most of the best practice institutions were standardizing on a single course authorware platform, such as WebCT or Blackboard. This made faculty training easier, reduced licensing costs, offered a consistent look and feel across different courses, and provided consistency for student use. There is a risk that this might limit different teaching approaches, but usually these authorware systems can be adapted or run in parallel with CD-ROM–based software such as Macromedia Director for special purposes.

Policies and Funding

Most of the seven best practice institutions have steadily moved toward strategic investments and firm criteria for funding instructional technology.

In the early stages of adoption of new technology for teaching, institutions tend to be more concerned with getting instructional technology projects started than with quality control. Thus many institutions when first getting into technology-based projects rely heavily on special funding and one-off grants, supporting individual, enthusiastic faculty. Twenty-one (60%) of the 35 universities and colleges indicated that the state legislature or system office had designated funds for faculty development related to technology in the most recent fiscal year.

However, most of the best practice institutions in this study had moved beyond this stage and were now assigning a significant portion of their base operating budget toward supporting instructional technology initiatives and faculty instructional development. Figures averaged around $1,000 to $1,500 per faculty member per annum for faculty development at a departmental level, and central funding for faculty development was in the $500,000 to $800,000 per annum, depending on the size of the institution.

The best-practice institutions had also set operational standards for the development of materials and support of students, and clear criteria for selecting projects for funding support. For instance, the California State University's statewide Commission on Learning Resources and Instructional Technology has developed "Standards and Criteria for Selecting Projects."

Many of the best practice institutions in this study and nearly all the educational institutions surveyed—30 out of 35, or 86%—participated in consortial or multiinstitutional activities related to faculty instructional development. Just over half of the 35 surveyed institutions (18) contracted with private companies or other institutions for either faculty development or the development of technology-based instructional materials. Twenty-two (63%) generate some form of revenue from technology-related instructional products, such as CD-ROMs, online courses, and developing materials for publishers. Partnerships took a number of forms:

- Arrangements with commercial publishers for the development of multimedia tools.

- Partnerships with business and industry representatives to develop courses and products that matched employers' needs.
- Partnership with nonprofit organizations that promote the use of technology in teaching.
- Partnerships or consortia of universities, colleges, and K–12 schools for sharing faculty development programs and resources.

The California State University's Center for Distributed Learning is a good example of a statewide partnership of institutions and also of partnership with the private sector through its agreement with the publisher Addison-Wesley-Longman.

The advantages of partnership and consortia are that they spread development costs over a wider range of users, they enable joint marketing of courses and products, and the risk of investment is shared and thus lessened. Also, there is a great deal of learning that takes place through partnerships that spreads the knowledge base more widely.

To summarize, external grants are invaluable for getting institutions initiated in new technology projects and for supporting projects when the projects are consistent with the overall strategic priorities of an institution. However, the best-practice institutions in this study are using their own base funding to ensure the sustainability of instructional technology and to ensure that it is consistent with the overall strategic directions and values of the institution.

Performance Measurement

This is probably the weakest part of the study. None of the best-practice institutions had tracked the relationship between the cost of technology-based teaching initiatives and any resulting benefits, and none had related investment in faculty instructional development to enhanced learning.

Institutions did have general student evaluation and peer-review processes in place. The University of Central Florida was in the middle of a faculty survey on the effectiveness of the online programs, and has data on student satisfaction showing that a combination of face-to-face and online teaching was preferred to either just face-to-face or solely online teaching (Dziuban et al., 1999). Virginia Tech conducts regular assessment studies of course development activities. The CSU Center for Distributed Learning does formative evaluation/user testing of its products.

In general, one has to go outside this study to projects such as the PBS/Annenburg Flashlight project and the Canadian NCE-Telelearning project (e.g., Bartolic-Zlomislic and Bates, 1999) to obtain data on the cost effectiveness of instructional technologies. There is certainly plenty of scope for more studies in this area, and in particular the relationship between investment in faculty instructional development and the effective use of learning technologies.

CONCLUSIONS

I want to recognize first of all the generosity of the seven best-practice institutions and the APQC in making these findings available to the general public. In an era in which there is increasing competition in higher education, the seven best-practice institutions have been enormously generous in sharing their practices with the sponsor organizations, and now through this publication with a much wider audience.

I do not think this point can be emphasized too strongly. Increasing competition from the private sector, and moves to commercialize educational activities, especially in the area of online learning, are making many organizations less willing to share their knowledge and experience. However, I am delighted to see that the spirit of collegiality and the willingness freely to share knowledge and experience is still alive and well in North America.

The study also brought home to me very forcibly that faculty development in instructional technology must be looked at in the context of the institution as a whole. I was much impressed with the "total immersion" approach to the use of technology by all the best-practice institutions. Although each institution is aware of the dangers and pitfalls of technology-based teaching, they have moved beyond the courtship stage into a fully committed relationship, and are responding to all that this entails. Faculty development in instructional technology is for most of them just one of many essential strategies for success. Fortunately this is also balanced by their recognition that teaching and learning have to drive technology, and not the other way round.

The study also clearly identified two fundamentally different approaches to faculty instructional development. Many institutions outside this study are expecting faculty members to pick up the necessary skills to use technology in the classroom for themselves, or are at best offering separate courses and workshops on information technology. This might include instructional design issues, as well as how to create a Web site. These workshops will be offered by specialist centralized faculty development staff and/or staff from the institutional computing division.

However, what has emerged from this study is a totally different approach. Faculty members work in multidisciplinary teams in which the faculty member concentrates on subject matter and the best ways to teach this (problem-based, discussion-based, etc.). Their faculty development in instruction is just-in-time learning embedded in actual teaching projects. Additional specialist workshops are available to those who are interested, but the primary aim is to get faculty members working in multidisciplinary teams. Best-practice institutions have taken this approach to ensure high quality and control faculty workload. A particular feature of best-practice institutions is their ability to work collaboratively across organizational boundaries to support faculty in their use of technology for teaching.

One should not be surprised by this development. Every change in technology from the wheel to wireless computing has required or resulted in fundamental changes in the way we work. The development of separate specialist units such as faculties and academic departments, faculty development offices, and distance education units reflects the older industrial model of organization. The newer postindustrial technologies require smaller, more flexible organizational structures based around job tasks, and multidisciplinary project teams are one response to this need.

Lastly, one pervading message came through to me from the case studies. Moving an institution into the intelligent use of new technologies for teaching is not an easy task. It requires a huge effort. It requires management committed to change, an understanding of the limitations as well as the benefits of teaching through technology, the willingness to make mistakes, and, even more important, the willingness to recognize that a mistake has been made and do something about it, faculty members committed to teaching and open to new ideas, a recognition that faculty members need adequate instructional and technical support and appropriate and substantive rewards for their efforts, and major reallocation of resources.

Moving an institution to the appropriate use of learning technologies is more about human change than about technical decisions, and hence requires patience and a long-term strategy. The institutions represented in these case studies all reflect these characteristics. What also comes through from the case studies is the excitement, commitment, and sense of achievement that this effort has brought.

These studies provide a rich source of information for instructors, leaders of higher education institutions, and students of higher education. Working with SHEEO, APQC, the sponsor institutions, and the best-practice partners has been one of my most pleasant and instructive work assignments. I hope this book captures the commitment, the idealism, and the experience of all those with whom I worked on this project.

REFERENCES

Bartolic-Zlomislic, S., and A. W. Bates. (1999). "Investing in On-line Learning: Potential Benefits and Limitations." *Canadian Journal of Communication* 24, pp. 349–366.

Bates, A.W. (2000). *Managing Technological Change: Strategies for College and University Leaders.* San Francisco: Jossey-Bass.

Dziuban, C., J. Hartman, F. Juge, P. Moskal, S. Sorg, and B. Truman-Davis. (1999). "Faculty Development, Learner Support and Evaluation in Web-Based Programs." *Interactive Learning Environments* (The Netherlands), 7, nos. 2 & 3, pp. 137–154.

INDEX